FOREWORD BY ALAN WEISS

AUTHOR OF *MILLION DOLLAR CONSULTING*

The Leader
Architect

THE RIGHT PEOPLE
IN THE RIGHT PLACES
DOING THE RIGHT STUFF
AT THE RIGHT TIME

Laurie & Alan,

Jim Grew

Best, Jim

CAREER PRESS

This edition first published in 2018 by
Career Press, an imprint of Red Wheel/Weiser, LLC
With offices at:
65 Parker Street, Suite 7
Newburyport, MA 01950
www.redwheelweiser.com
www.careerpress.com

ISBN: 978-1-63265-133-4
Library of Congress Cataloging-in-Publication Data
available upon request.

Cover design by Ty Nowicki
Interior by Lauren Manoy
Typeset in Optima and D-DIN Condensed

Printed in Canada
MAR
10 9 8 7 6 5 4 3 2 1

Praise for *The Leader Architect:*

"If you lead people, keep this book on your desk. It will help you up your game quickly, with practical ideas that are easy to use."
—Robert MacLellan, cofounder, Pacific Restaurants

"Filled with useful applications of business theory, the book gives you numerous ways to continuously improve what you do. *The Leader Architect* is a terrific book for those looking for how to succeed with their business."
—Norm Duffett, president, Orca Capital Securities, LLC

"Utilizing an engaging mix of case studies, examples, anecdotes and how-to's, Jim Grew presents management strategies and tactics sure to propel any business to the next level."
—Jason M. Brauser, partner, STOEL RIVES LLP

"I've been involved in investing in over 100 startup companies and have participated on the boards of about fifty. Without exception every one of these companies would have benefited greatly from the insights presented in the very readable and understandable form in this exceptional book."
—Elwood Howse, cofounder, Cable & Howse Ventures

"I could always determine if the plant was profitable just by walking through it. That gut report doesn't translate well to managers, as talented and insightful as they may be. What they found indispensable was Jim Grew's concept of a scoreboard."
—Don Jones, chairman and cofounder, JVNW Inc.

"Jim Grew's unique insights will help to not only empower teams, but also turn executives into leaders."
—Scott Showalter, president and CEO, Oregon Symphony

"*The Leader Architect* is the proof of why Jim is called the Defogger and Accelerator. The chapter on Myths is a case in point. I told my clients that the practical advice in this chapter alone made the book my Christmas gift to them. Every page teems with pragmatic advice based on real world experience."
—Jerry Fletcher, CEO, Z-axis Marketing, Inc

"The impact of Jim's book on our business was immediate. His results-oriented approach and wisdom were just what we needed to get our company to the next level. Jim's insights and guidance were invaluable."

—Hal Cranston, chairman and cofounder
Emerald Landscape Co. Inc.

"Jim Grew is truly the 'Leader Architect' by the way he lays out the structure and foundational principles necessary to be an effective leader. He has an uncanny ability to quickly drill down to the critical elements that help organizations hire and develop high-functioning players."

—Don Bielen, Principal Perkins & Co.

"Jim Grew has a great ability to listen and in listening he has acquired a great insight to how people and organizations work. Because of his experience in *The Leader Architect* he shows that there is a wide array of definitions of 'success' and sets his solutions in the context of the client's definition."

—David Williams, retired CEO, ShoreBank Pacific

"*The Leader Architect* makes available to business owners like me the performance metrics and management efficiencies that Jim used to help us to significantly grow the profitability of our construction group."

—Bill Mascott, owner, Mascott Equipment Co.

"Small- to medium-sized business leaders are trapped by the countless constraints inherent in running small enterprises. *The Leader Architect* addresses these constraints and provides new insights, new ways of thinking and a new perspective on what is otherwise well-travelled ideas providing a key to break free of the trap leaders find themselves in."

—David DeMots, CEO, Package Containers, Inc.,
CEO, DHX Advertising, Inc.

"Jim Grew's book is a blueprint of how to understand, delegate and motivate the people in your organization. By understanding this blueprint, you can become your own leader architect."

—Laura Markee, founder and president, Markee Valuations

Contents

Foreword

Small- to medium-sized enterprises (SMEs) generate all—*100 percent*—of net new jobs in North America. Counterintuitively, perhaps, large firms do not. They mostly either merely replace existing jobs, or they reduce jobs through automation and outsourcing overseas. IBM, Boeing, Microsoft, and 3M are not producing new jobs and new employment.

But those businesses on Main Street, in the suburban malls, and on the exurban campuses, are. These firms are often closely held, and some are in the same families for decades. Some are start-ups with stars in their eyes. Some are franchises and local outlets.

All of them require a particular kind of care and feeding because they can't afford to make major errors; a small business could be sunk by a half-million-dollar mistake, whereas the likes of a Prudential or Pfizer would hardly notice a ten-million-dollar mistake. Family dynamics—from cousins on the payroll to children who need a college fund—play a role in investment far different from the considerations of a senior manager at Hewlett-Packard or Merck.

"Small" doesn't mean "easy." There are fewer resources, more intense competition, greater technological issues, and, most of all, far greater challenges with people, from motivation to retention, from lack of opportunity to poor performance. As a consultant for more than thirty years, I've found that smaller businesses have greater challenges than their larger cousins, with a far shorter life expectancy.

Thus it's more than refreshing—it's salvation—that Jim Grew, one of the foremost authorities on SME performance and profit in the country, has found the time to record his insights, experiences, and resultant advice in *The Leader Architect*. I know of no other work that comprehensively and authoritatively examines the professional and personal challenges of leading a successful small business in these volatile times.

Read this wonderful book carefully. This architect sheds light on your surroundings, constructs a solid foundation, and enables you to enjoy the house you're building every day.

—Alan Weiss, PhD
Author, *Million Dollar Consulting, Threescore and More,* and more than sixty other books

Introduction

This book is the reverse of most business leadership or management books. Instead of exploring the depths of particular theories and structures for success, this book bridges the chasm between what to do and how to do it for senior business executives. It offers ample theoretical foundations for the key management and leadership tasks these executives face, but provides clear and specific guidance about how and when to apply these powerful theories. It is especially for owners and CEOs, whose task is to lead successful growth in the face of a blizzard of advice. For simplicity, we'll use "leadership" for both leadership and management.

We move beyond advocating for growth alone, looking past earnings and net worth toward the true measure of a business: its value in the marketplace. That value is dramatically impacted by the experience of its customers and employees, which determines its ability to endure.

You haven't read this book yet, in spite of its promise to explore both leadership and improved organizational outcomes—evergreen themes for sure. (When we talk about "businesses," we mean any organization of more than six people, where the leader can't keep her hands on all that goes on.) Here's what's different:

1. A higher measure of success: valuation of the business.

2. More practical application than theory of what to do.

3. A deeper focus on what produces success: human behavior, or what the people in the business choose to do or not do.

4. A carefully selected collection of structures and processes to help people do what success demands.

5. A pragmatic combination of immediately useful techniques and a range of theoretical templates covering the most vital topics facing leaders today.

This mix offers a faster answer to the perennial leadership question: What can I do with the time and resources available to deliver what's important for our organization? It's a survey course with chops, combining tools and guidelines for immediate application. It's deep enough to be effective, and broad enough to cover most of the prime topics for success. It provides enough theory to apply to most of the organizational situations that a leader will encounter. (Not that you should stop reading, but this will provide a foundation to build your own leadership practice as you raise the targets of your business.)

Chapter 1

The Myths that Ruin Our Businesses

The four Kerry Blue Terriers looked identical. All were out for a walk in an open field with their owner. Three of the dogs bounded joyously about, reveling in the moment. The fourth ran in circles, relentlessly. Why? The owner explained that when he acquired the fourth dog, it had been living in a cage. For years, its exercise was running in a circle limited by the cage.[1] The cage was long gone, but the dog remained inside it, at least in its mind. That invisible, powerful story guided the dog's perception of reality, and its life. Myth, indeed!

As a leader, how do you change the behavior of the fourth dog on your team?

We are pattern-seekers from birth, making sense of our environment. Doubt it? Videos of days-old babies show pattern-seeking. Crying begins as a hunger reflex, but toddlers shift to crying on demand, having learned that crying produces food, cuddles, attention. Our brains sort billions of stimuli from outside, ignoring most and processing few. More important, what do we do with the things we sort? They become our personal myths!

What is the link from patterns to myths? When we take in a bit of data, we apply our own meaning based on our experience, genetic heritage, and what we learn from reading and other things. Our meanings become our myths.

Now, wait a minute. It doesn't really matter whether our myths are true or not. Truth is not the test, because "truth" is "out there." I see the sun moving from east to west every day, and in spite of knowing that our Earth moves, not the sun, I think (and feel) that the sun moves. Remarkably, that bit of error is a useful myth; it guides everything from which sides of the house require window shades to when we decide to put on sunscreen.

Myths are the guardrails on the paths of our lives. We put them there, often not realizing that we're letting them guide us. We all have myths that help us manage the peril and possibilities of the future.

Starting when I was ten years old, we spent our summers at a cabin in the woods in the Columbia River Gorge in Washington State. The woods were full of plants, bushes, bugs, frogs, and even bears (we found a bear print once and made a plaster of Paris casting of it for proof). We connected with other folks by boat or trail, usually trail, because our parents had first call on the boat. We ran the trail over and over every day, meeting our friends to play Kick the Can, go to the swim dock, play Hide and Seek, and other essential kid stuff. Finally, we found that we could walk the trail at night without a flashlight: signal achievement! We did it by feeling the trail with our feet because it was pitch black outside.

Here's how our myth was built:

1. Walk the trail hundreds of times.

2. Notice that we could feel the little holes, dips, roots, and rocks with our feet.

3. Try it in the dark with a flashlight.

4. Turn off the light and try it for a bit.

5. Eureka! We "saw" without a light.

Where's the myth? The belief that we could "see" the trail and find our way home in the darkest dark. We did find our way home (it worked), but we didn't "see" at all.

By now you're starting to see that you carry hundreds of myths with you through your life, adding and dropping them as your experience grows. Experience in our context includes both physical experience and mental experience, because both impact our myths and choices. Your memory of Nelson Mandela from a movie can generate strong feelings much later, perhaps while viewing news of a public riot in the United States. Your memory is a myth built by your mind as you experienced the story of Mandela—despite never meeting him in person.

Why do we hang on to myths?

◊   Powerful emotions are linked to them.

◊   We have a sense of control as we deal with frightening life setbacks.

◊   They are affirmations of important values in a struggle about what is right to do.

◊   They offer protection from confusion and dread as we look into an unclear future.

◊   They offer encouragement to try something new.

We believe in myths because we need them to live our lives. Let's just use the results of intensive brain and behavior study, especially the past fifty years, and call our perceptions "myths." These myths, and many like them, lubricate the gears of our life and are reinforced frequently, making them seem even truer. If you begin to observe your perceptions, you'll see the web that allows you to move through your life mostly efficiently: the connective tissue between your brain and the world. Otherwise, you'd get bogged down when you reach for the water faucet.

In our brains, the more a connection between synapses is used, the more we think it's true. "Knowledge" is synaptic connection in our heads. Sometimes it's scientifically verified by outside data, but other times, it's verified by our feelings.

Sisyphus, Greek king of Corinth (known then as Ephyra), was self-serving, crafty, and deceitful. Zeus, king of the gods, punished him by forcing him to roll a huge boulder to the top of a long hill. Exhausted, he watched helplessly as the boulder rolled back down the hill to the bottom, forcing a do-over. He could never quite make it to the top. Today, we refer to long, arduous tasks (like owning a midsize business) that seem never-ending as "Sisyphean" tasks.

The myth has lived on for thousands of years because it's a fitting metaphor for a common life experience. If you're the one doing the endless tough work, it can feel so familiar that it seems true. And for you, it is, conjuring up a picture about your life that's rich in detail and feelings.

Myths are superb tools to communicate complex ideas with others who know the myth. A myth is a metaphor on steroids, boosted because it describes an experience and the feelings that go with it.

MOST COMMON AND DANGEROUS MYTHS

The people in your organization, the folks that you rely on to make things work, are as full of myths as you are. And some of their myths are different from yours. And they aren't telling you any more about their myths than you tell them about your myths. And, in fact, most of their actions are driven by those invisible myths. This means that your leadership is mostly about guiding their myths and helping to create new myths in the process. The challenge, however, is that they—and you—carry myths that are both untrue and dangerous to your organization. Even more dangerous, they are seldom mentioned, let alone discussed or tested.

Here are some commonly held and dangerous myths. Each is wrong, and hazardous to your health and your business. Which of these are familiar to you?

Myth 1: Bosses Lie, and They Care Only About Themselves

This is true of some bosses, and smart people leave those bosses immediately. Most other bosses truly care about their organization's success, which helps their people make a living and learn new skills.

A company that I work with hit hard times in 2009, laying off most of its employees and draining the savings of the owners. The owner teared up as he described laying off fifteen-year employees. His face lit up as he described the joy of bringing them back to the company when sales improved. This story is about his face, not the employees. In fact, one of his prime concerns about his kids taking over the business is whether they have the same powerful empathy for their people (employees).

> *I am an old man now, and I have had a great many problems. Most of them never happened.*
>
> —*Mark Twain*

Myth 2: Process Improvement Beats Teamwork

The genius of process improvement is that process changes are independent of the people doing the work. Workers can be brought in from outside the process, and the process is available for them to implement.

The curse of process improvement is that it depends on the people to do the work the new and better way. Increased efficiency usually requires acute attention to detail, which comes either from years of experience or careful teaching. The reasons that process improvements don't stick are almost always about the people, not the process.

I worked at a loudspeaker manufacturing firm where the team lead turned the idea of process improvement into a game with his people. He played the game with me on my daily plant tour. I'd ask, "What's the improvement today?" He'd always have one. Always. More remarkably, most of the ideas came from his team, not engineers or outside analysts. I tell you this, not to push the tired meme that "the people know" (because just as often they don't), but because their leader turned their work into a game that gave them recognition every day. On the days where there was no improvement idea, he'd still ask about it, keeping it alive for the next day. Their work was way past following someone else's process rules; they loved the challenge of finding a better way. Oh, and their quality and efficiency rose to record levels!

Myth 3: Inputs Are More Important than Outputs

Activity untethered to results frequently produces frantic action but no change. The worst example of this was an otherwise skilled production manager growling, "I want to see all the machines going up and down for the whole shift." The result was that welders (the second step in the process) hiked all over the plant to find the next pallet of parts to assemble and weld. They were told that their slow welding was making the machines wait! Actually, what made the machines wait was a sloppy work schedule in the first production process in the plant. That process was laser cutting, and the guy leading the laser team grabbed the simplest job in the pile to do next, instead of choosing jobs to optimize plant throughput. When the schedule changed at the laser, the welders stopped walking and went back to welding, which they preferred. Both problem and solution were about the team lead's choice regarding work schedule. It was not about the process.

If people are rewarded for what they do, instead of for their results, it can produce a gauzy happiness with calls made, units produced, orders shipped, and so forth. An e-commerce client found customer call-backs rising, a sign of increasing customer dissatisfaction. Instead of scheduling more folks to handle the call-backs (more activity), the COO adjusted scheduling so that more people were available at peak call times. Call-backs dropped back into an acceptable range without adding people. More important, they took care of customers on time.

Myth 4: Analysis Beats Individual Behavior

Noise about benchmarking and big data obscures the reality that skilled sales people or internal leaders may find an 80 percent solution quickly, and delivering that solution produces progress and a sharper point on the next step to success. Most of the time, analysis feels good but doesn't speed the process of delivering real help to customers. It just reduces stress inside the company. Sometimes a beer is better.

Myth 5: Plans Before Execution Beats Execution to Build Plans

Although there are times that good plans beat execution, usually rapid execution will clarify needed adjustment to plans more quickly and precisely. This approach requires a sensitive balance of listening to customers and a willingness to adjust. It comes by watching customer results, not progress versus plans.

Myth 6: Metrics Provide Accountability

The power of good metrics is focus. Without commitment built on accountability, however, metrics soon lose their punch. A manufacturing company designed new metrics, carefully explained their sources, and posted them daily. One day, I asked the production manager what he thought of the metrics (they were aimed at him). He pointed to the executive conference room and said, "It's up to them!" His message confirmed that the correct data hadn't laid a glove on him, and he felt no accountability at all. As good as the numbers were, what was missing was the conversation with him about his role in moving the numbers and what it meant to the future of the company.

Myth 7: Exceeding Expectations
Beats Meeting Goals

"Exceeding expectations" is lazy leadership, meant to substitute for crisp objectives about things that matter to employees, suppliers, and customers. The myth is that hefty promises pull top results with them. The reverse is usually the case, as explained by a veteran middle manager in a privately owned production firm: "We never had goals. The owner just said that he knew we could do better, as he called us to 'exceed our customer's expectations,' whatever that meant. What it meant to me was that we always fell short, no matter how hard we worked. It was a real downer."

Myth 8: If You Put the Right People in the Right Jobs and Leave Them Alone, They'll Excel

This error comes from the well-meaning leader who has successfully built a thriving business from scratch. With growth and complexity come an escalating requirement for blunt communication and teamwork.

Being an able leader doesn't translate to making the right decisions in the high-speed complexity that marks all successful firms. Instead, preplanned processes and connections help folks to work together to get the right stuff done.

Myth 9: A Strong Leader Is More Effective than Delegation to a Team

This is true when the organization is small enough for the leader to know what everyone is doing. It's also true in times of extreme change (high growth, slumping sales, or a merger with another organization) for a short time (months). If the strong leader devotes herself to building a strong team early, the momentum of change can be amplified with improving quality. The secret is in the leader shifting focus to team effectiveness, instead of business effectiveness. If the leader insists on leading himself, the capacity of the business to grow will be truncated. High-growth markets will hide the limits of a strong leader, but competition or the eventual shift to moderate growth will slow business growth.

Myth 10: Department Excellence Beats Teamwork Across Departments

The basic truth is that all departments should have a hand in company success, or they should be disbanded. When there are fewer than twenty employees or so, communication is common unless there's a catastrophic personal collision. Folks see each other daily, and it's easy to keep up with each other in the course of walking around. Beyond twenty people, misunderstandings spike, regardless of motivation, style, or skill. The culprit is the very department targets that led to excellence. Folks are trained to do the core work of the department before anything else. The flow of work, praise, and job security is a flood of department tasks, with occasional links to other teams floating in the river like debris. Doubt it? Look around your office at lunchtime. How many folks are eating at their desks? Their vote is to spend their time on those tasks, not on other people, even though talking with those people would likely make their jobs easier or their results better.

Unless there is a mechanism for regular communication, silo thinking sprouts, even in companies with a hundred employees. That communication mechanism has to be automatic, simple, and clearly useful, or good employees will ignore it. The mechanism seldom is money. Instead, recognition and structured work time can enable it.

Myth 11: Bonuses Should Be Individually Crafted to Fit Each Department

This crazy notion feeds on the idea that folks in each department need special skills, so their bonuses must be individualized. But it's wasteful: Incentives should be tied to clear results, not individual skills. This is the signing bonus gone awry. If extra skills or work don't benefit customers and the company goals, it is waste and should stop.

The truth is that because all departments (and people) are needed for success in the company, measuring individual contribution is necessary but insufficient for calculating incentive pay. Instead, incentives linked to total company performance will pull your best people into working together for both pride and profit. Such teamwork doesn't require paying everyone the same, although that's successfully done in some firms.

One successful way to do that is to build a company bonus pool as a percentage of earnings, then allocate the pool based upon a mix of individual factors including salary or performance against objectives. It's relatively easy to show that all employee compensation rises as the pool enlarges, and quarterly pool reporting and public formulas for calculating the pool each month enable employees to calculate their personal bonus fund's growth.

Counterintuitively, because most successful sales people are "coin-operated," their bonuses should be tied to their performance, calculated separately from the rest of the company, but paid from the company pool and reported (if not paid) quarterly or monthly.

How We Achieve Myth Relief

Why bother with myth relief? Myths can impact the present and the future, so like putting steering wheels on cars, we'd like to set aside the dangerous myths before a damaging collision occurs.

Remember the four dogs? Three dogs knew they were running in a field, and the fourth dog acted like it was still in its cage. The difference was in their myths, wasn't it? Imagine if 25 percent of your people thought that the goal was profit at all costs, customer be damned! Those 25 percent create a riptide that dangerously slows your whole operation, like a surfer trying mightily to get past the rip and out to where the riding waves are. By the time she gets there, she's out of energy, and the next rides are lousy. And no one wants to be in the 25 percent that's aiming the wrong way!

Yes, that fourth dog is neurotic. A neurosis is an unconscious false belief about the world that seems real to its user. A false belief lives and has power because it's useful and satisfying, and the more it's invoked, the stronger it becomes. It also blocks a clear view of reality, when reality and neurosis clash. You, dear reader, are participating in this discussion with the neurotic belief that you don't have neurotic beliefs. Of course you do, on a range of topics. Much of the time they do little damage; sometimes they help (little white lies, for example), and sometimes they send you down the road to failure—at least for the task at hand.

If my myths mislead me, and your myths mislead you, then our company is full of people who are misled to some extent. These stories won't go away, but they can be powered down and allowed to linger at the side, untended.

As you might expect, there's a three-step process for myth relief:

1. Identify them (the hardest part).

2. Rate their danger potential.

3. Erase or defang the most damaging.

Learn Your Personal Myths

Your personal myths are also called your cognitive bias. "Cognitive bias" is described by Richard L. Byyny, MD, as "a systematic pattern of deviation from norm or rationality in judgment, whereby inferences about other people and situations may be drawn in an illogical fashion. Individuals create their own 'subjective social reality' from their perception of the input."[2] These are often unconscious beliefs that a person isn't aware of and doesn't question, but that provide powerful guidance in behavior, judgments, and relationships. Sounds a lot like myths.

When you find yourself acting on a belief that defies available data, pay attention to the quiet alarms in your head or on your colleagues' faces: likely there's a personal myth operating. Look at the data to see if you should drop it, modify it, or keep it. And sometimes there is no data check available, but the smart person stays open to the possibility that even cherished beliefs defended loudly may be untrue. Here's a simple personal myth check (no peeking): What percentage of Americans are vegetarians? *Answer at the end of this section.

Why look for your own myths? Myth energy can be so strong that consciously aiming it can make a striking difference in your life, happiness, effectiveness, relationships, and more. Aiming is no more than spotting a myth in action and doing the data check. If it's real, move along; nothing to see here. If it's questionable, ask if it matters to anything that you care about (your values, your company's success, the well-being of your friends or family, etc.). If yes, rebuild the myth on the data, and change what you're doing. If no, ignore it, and especially stop sharing it with others.

No one gets it all the time, but like the old baseball analogy, getting it right a third of the time pulls you out of an eddy of waste in your life.

Company Myth Finder

Answer quickly and honestly. It's your company, after all. Rate how each sentence below applies to your company now. Write your score on a separate sheet of paper using the following scale. If there's a myth that you think deserves attention but it's not listed, write it down.

1 = Seldom 2 = Sometimes 3 = Frequently

4 = Mostly 5 = Always

1. Bosses lie, and they care only about themselves.
2. Process improvement beats teamwork.
3. Inputs are more important than outputs.
4. Analysis beats individual behavior.
5. Execution before plans beats good plans before execution.
6. Metrics provide accountability.
7. Exceeding expectations beats meeting goals.
8. If you put the right people in the right jobs and leave them alone, they'll excel.

9. A strong leader is more effective than delegation to a team.

10. Department excellence beats teamwork across departments.

11. Bonuses should be individually crafted to fit each department.

12. I know I'm doing a good job because no one has chewed me out.

13. Other [fill in the blank].

Ways to Use This Data

◊ Add suspected myths to the list.

◊ Ask key leaders and employees at all levels to fill out the Myth Finder.

◊ Send responses it to a neutral person to tally and summarize.

◊ Schedule a sixty-minute work session to discuss questions like these:

> » What are the three most damaging myths?

> » Which is the strongest (believed by the most people)?

> » What are the facts to counter this myth?

> » How do we communicate those facts?

> » Do they justify a workshop approach? Present findings, present facts, discuss, and ask for actions outside the room. Use a workshop approach when the facts are either complex

or unlikely to be believed (or cared about) if simply recited in a company communication (letter, talk at meeting, e-broadcast).

» Do we need a regular de-mything process in the company?

Pay Attention to Behavior

Where you see behavior that doesn't fit the data as you know it, do one of two things:

◊　Get the best data you can find to clarify reality.

◊　Ask the person what prompted them to do it.

If the data is unconvincing, then direct interviews will usually uncover the myth. With either tool, remind yourself that you're seeking what's real, even if it's not what you believe or prefer. The practice of seeking evidence will dissolve myths by itself, as it's observed by others. The truth may not set you free, but its power to simplify can be breathtaking.

For example, dramatic cuts in reimbursements endangered a chain of physical therapy clinics. They recovered by intensive myth-busting.

Myth: Therapists believed that revenue increases would require them to speed up. That would endanger patient satisfaction and treatment quality, the basis of physician referrals.

Myth-buster: When therapist treatment hours and patient satisfaction were posted daily in each clinic, therapists sought ways to move their results. When the therapists saw that they could get more patients to come to treatment just by helping them understand the treatment and asking how they were doing (relationship), their efficiency and cash flow improved dramatically— along with an increase in patient happiness (they measured it).

Replace Negative Myths with a DAC System

As you start noticing myths, go ahead and sort them into two piles: helpful and not helpful. This sort can be quick and easy so that you know which myths to reinforce with measuring or recognition, and which need to be stopped or changed.

Replace negative myths with a data, action, and communication (DAC) system. The core of this system is real-time data shared broadly and frequently in team settings whose purpose is to frame its individual responses. Its purpose is to shift all employees' evaluation of what they need to do from their myths to actions built on a reality system. (There's more on the DAC system in Chapter 3.)

*Answer to special question: 3 percent of Americans are vegetarian.[3]

Changing Our Beliefs into Vision

I learned to windsurf with my thirteen-year-old nephew— in Kansas. He moved to Maui and became one of the top professional freestyle windsurfers in the world; I did not. With his windsurfing gear, he sails a wave, launches as much as twenty feet in the air to do aerobatics, and lands back on the wave. Like all acrobats (gymnasts, ice skaters, divers) he learns his moves like this:

◊ Picture each step.

◊ Try it.

◊ Clarify the picture.

◊ Rinse and repeat—hundreds of times.

Yes, his moves are a string of pictures in his mind. His head moves toward the pictures in sequence, and his body and windsurfing gear follow. His pictures are his "vision." It has pulled him from a kid in Kansas to a world-ranked competitor in an extreme sport.

A vision is a picture of the future. The best are emotional and specific. Done right, it can power a great organization by aligning people's emotions, analysis, and actions toward the same end. It's a common concept that's seldom used well, if at all, because it's easy to create and hard to live daily.

Stanford professor David Cheriton and Sun Microsystems cofounder Andy Bechtolsheim met on David's porch in Palo Alto in 1998 to hear the ideas of Larry Page and Sergey Brin about their page-rank algorithm. Those ideas vaulted into a vision so compelling that Andy ran to his car to get his checkbook. He and David each wrote a check for $100,000 to Brin and Page, becoming the first major investors in a company that became known as Google. That $100,000 has grown to more than $1 billion.

What was that vision? It was access to mind-bending amounts of information instantly for everyday users, including students writing a term paper. Its basis was a switching technology orders of magnitude faster than anything then available. Dr. Cheriton says he has "a belief that if you are providing real value to the world and doing it in a sensible way, then the market rewards you."[4]

There's the vision: It's not's the faster switch; it's the instant access to information for millions of people.

It's easy to stop at the billions in value at Google. The point is the power of the vision, however, because it ignited a future beyond imagination. Without the vision, powered by David's deep knowledge of switching algorithms, there's no explosion of technology. This process mirrors the power of vision. Vision correctly used literally means to make a picture of our organization's output in the future, exploding like the Big Bang. Don't miss the "exploding" part. That's numbers of people who were captivated enough to move toward that vision, and their captivation became Google!

What's myth got to do with vision? Myths provide these three essentials for folks who are serious about reaching their picture or their vision:

◊   Myths (beliefs) often carry a knockout punch of energy, essential for the slog to the finish line of each part of your vision. My nephew can see himself doing his entire move—a complex ballet in the sky with windsurf gear attached and coral reef in a foot of water below. That picture picks him up when he falls and sails him out to try again.

◊   Myths help you drop activities that don't move you toward your picture.

◊   Myths help you create a compelling vision that you can't wait to experience. My nephew would say that pulling off the move fifteen feet above the water and landing back on the wave is a rush that defies description. The myth is that he has already done it; the experience is his addiction, and he can't wait to try it again.

WHY HAVE A VISION?

An organization is a group of myths trying to go somewhere together. Each of us is a bundle of myths squinting into the daylight to find our paths. The first function of a company vision statement is to corral the hundreds of myths running around via its employees, and aim enough of them in the same direction to enable positive movement. A vision can be the laser-like alignment that winning organizations and teams need for sustained success.

Myths Drive Future Outcomes

In fact, the power of myths is that we use them to help control our future. The very uncertainty of the future is both a curse and a gift, depending on your personal myths. The outcome of an organization is powerfully impacted by its myths and their translation into personal myths by its people. That personal translation becomes the myth of each employee, powerfully driving individual behavior, and by extension, the performance of the organization.

So we live among two sets of myths: organizational and personal. Each myth set is impacted by past and present, as well as the other myth set, so it's no wonder that we're sometimes unclear about our myths. As an employee, my behavior at work is impacted by my myths and company myths, as I understand them. Myths are a powerful driver of company performance, culture, and aspirations. That swirl of myths can either be a laser or a lightbulb, depending on how leadership directs it.

How to Harness Myth/Vision Power

Sadly, the word "vision" is so overused it's like yesterday's coffee: dark, bad-smelling, and offering an unpleasant diversion from today's opportunities. Picture a
vision statement (if you can remember one) from an organization. Too often, it is standard words in a standard
frame in a standard place that sleeps like a Harry Potter
painting. But the vision doesn't come to life. Ever.

How do you bring your vision to life? Invite your
people to hop on the train that's going toward the vision. Their myths and wishes painted that vision picture
because they want to go there, so make it explicit.

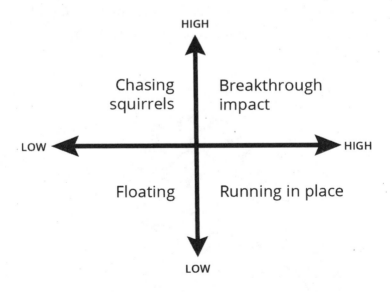

For example, we can harness the myth-building
strength of our people toward our purpose and create

powerful new myths about our value story by asking questions like these:

◊   What could we do for our customers?

◊   What is the value of each product or service?

◊   Will the value support a price that our customers will pay?

◊   How do we refine the value and our costs into a model that works for all of us?

◊   What value story can we create for our employees and our customers?

Yes, the "value story" is a myth, but a constructive one. It moves from story to myth as your employees live it, struggling with the hidden problems, reveling in the surprising satisfactions—and telling stories about problems solved and customers served in group discussion.

When you combine a myth-charged vision with a value-story myth for your organization, you've created a view of the present and the future that your employees can be excited about. Like our windsurfer, the gleam in their eyes is fueled by myths that they've chosen, and they want to be back on the wave as soon as possible.

Chapter 2

The Power of Pairs

This chapter will shift the focus from teamwork, which is common, to working in pairs, which is the connective tissue of winning organizations. Pairs are hidden in plain sight. Much is made of teams in organizations, sports, work groups, school classes, and so forth, but the pairs in the groups are seldom noted. Those pairs offer remarkable leverage to their teams, and to their individual members as well. Why is it that descriptions of teams often talk about pairs (catcher–pitcher; quarterback–receiver; research partners; writing partners) as they analyze success or failure?

Pairs are our most familiar relationship, perhaps because we often begin bonding with a parent within hours after we're born, even before we're aware of it. The strength of that bond can be a major source of emotional strength through life. That attachment is so familiar, and so vital, that it's no surprise that pairs remain a source of powerful emotional connection.[1]

Pairs, or dyads, offer the strongest emotional connection but are the least stable of all group sizes: If one member departs, the dyad ends. German sociologist Georg Simmel (1858–1918) discussed the relationship of group size and group dynamics. In summary, the larger the group, the more stable, but less emotionally connected; the smaller the group, the less stable, and the stronger the emotional connection. To test this, consider your emotional connection to your spouse or partner as compared to your emotional connection to your work group. The fact that this exists in plain sight doesn't hide its power, however.[2]

Now you know why so much is made of team building. Some pairs in a group will have such powerful

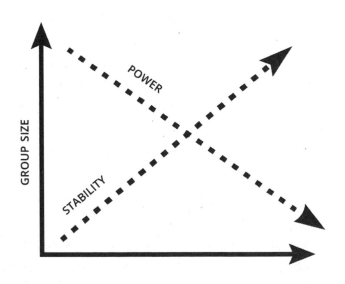

connections that their behaviors will lean toward each other, instead of group goals. Why not reverse this? Instead of focusing only on the team, why not focus on the power of pairs in the group as well? The deep emotional power of pairs can be a remarkable source of good in groups and in the organization. It can also be a powerful block to progress if not managed effectively.

Consider that in a group of eight, there are fifty-six pairs of people in relationship with each other. The connections aren't all of the same strength, of course, but their existence underlines the power and challenge of successfully leading a group. Why not recruit the power of pairs to boost the effectiveness of any group in an organization?

Empowering pairs can be most effective in strong groups, often characterized by shared goals, frequent feedback on performance, and the fact that success demands all of the team, not just a few. The undesirable opposite of a successful team is a group dominated by one or two "A" players who act like their performance confers power, recognition, and a senior place in the organization. "Taking the team to the next level" can become a reality instead of a tired cliché by empowering the natural pairs in the group. Their stronger emotional bond can power enhanced commitment and performance, within group goals.

It is a myth that most leadership work happens in groups. Some does, of course, but much coaching, direction, evaluation, and teaching happens between two people, such as a team lead teaching a work technique to an employee, a supervisor helping a manager clarify priorities for the coming week or month, and so forth. These interactions are a significant source of skill-building among managers and are a primary determinant of attitudes, including motivation and feelings of safety, risk, and appreciation. For example, the experiences of self-actualization and recognition can be much more powerful motivators than the modest increases in salary or bonuses available to most employees.

LINKING PEOPLE EFFECTIVELY

Since pairs can affect each other so powerfully, why not take advantage of strong relationships that already exist, and work to reduce the forces that push them apart? Begin by rating pair relationships by using this pair strength measure:

◊ Strong pair—1

◊ Negative pair (dislike each other, or one likes but the other dislikes)—2

◊ Neutral—3

Start with your leadership team because their impact is immense on the organization. List each member. Then pair each member with every other member of the team, one pair at a time. Observe their behavior in meetings and ask these questions:

1. Who is always supported by whom?

2. Who chooses to work with whom?

3. Who avoids whom?

4. Who fights with whom?

Use your ratings to find strong pairs and pairs that work together poorly.

Next, perform a confidential Individual Trust Audit on your leadership team, using a trusted outsider. Ask each person to rate every other person on a scale like the following example in Figure 2.2.

Instructions: Rate each person in the group on how much you trust them, using a scale where 1 = I don't trust them, and 5 = I thoroughly trust them.

Individual Trust Audit Example

NAME OF RATER: VALERIE		
Name of other person:	Jason	Rating: 4
Name of other person:	Anne	Rating: 3
Name of other person:	William	Rating: 5
Name of other person:	Gwen	Rating: 5
Name of other person:	David	Rating: 2

Note: Visit *grewco.com* to download Individual Trust Audit forms to use with your team.

Use the Want–Give Review as a discussion opener to begin fostering trust among pairs in a group or team.

The form is available for download on my website (grewco. com), and Figure 2.3 on this page illustrates an example.

Ask each person to fill out both columns. Group in pairs to discuss their answers with each other for seven minutes. Rotate pairs to cover all combinations in the group. For added impact, bring the group back together. Ask each person to share one positive idea that came from the exercise. In six months or a year, repeat the exercise with the same team. Ask each group member to share a significant change from the earlier exercise.

Want–Give Review Example

NAME: LANCE		
NAME	**I WANT**	**I WILL GIVE**
Phil	Let me explain before you interrupt.	Be on time to meetings.
Susan	Give me an example of your idea.	Listen to the discussion before offering changes.
Sara	Talk with me before you talk with your people.	Schedule our meetings ahead of time.

For strong pairs, assign leadership of initiatives that have a high-value, short time horizon, such as:

◊   Complex initiatives between departments.

◊   Modeling processes to be copied by others.

◊   Process improvements.

◊   Prototyping management of new initiatives.

◊   Developing high-potential junior executives by working together (make development explicit).

◊   Accelerating product development.

◊   Modeling examples of improved presentations to others, such as customers, process teams, other executives.

For negative pairs, when assigning projects or ad hoc work, either avoid putting these folks on the same team, or make the team at least five people to dilute their impact on each other.

Work to reduce negative perceptions:

◊   Interview each person separately about perceptions about the other.

◊   Share the interview with the person described.

◊   Modify the perceptions of each person with your own experience.

◊   Add positive characteristics that you see.

◊   Invite response, looking for willingness to improve in a specific area.

If you observe that this exercise doesn't reduce friction to an acceptable level, counsel each person individually about the impact their behavior has on the team and the company. If necessary, move one or both to other positions, or remove them from the firm. The message, sent by example, is that the company values working constructively with each other, even when friction occurs.

THE EMPATHY CONNECTION

Empathy is such a critical leadership tool that we'll pause to learn about it, learn how to expand your own empathy, and how to use it to improve your leadership.

Empathy is not weakness or emotional diversion. It's an essential skill for any leader, or any person seeking to work or relate constructively with another person. "No less a hard-muscled body than the US Army, in its *Army Field Manual on Leader Development* (one of the best resources on leadership I've ever seen) insists repeatedly that empathy is essential for competent leadership," says psychiatrist, psychoanalyst, and leadership expert Prudy Gourgechon, MD.[3]

Let's clarify what empathy is because it's one of those words that is commonly used incorrectly. It's the ability to put yourself in another person's shoes to understand their reaction. The tricky part is that it means putting yourself in their shoes and understanding how they would react in their shoes, not your shoes. Most of us confidently assume that we know how another is reacting because we put *them* in *our* shoes: backward and often way off the mark.

Empathy is "knowing (and usually sharing) the other person's experience, perspective, and feelings."[4] It may or may not include your own feelings. This "knowing" means that you can imagine what's going on in the other person's thoughts and feelings, although imperfectly. It is a "neutral data gathering tool"[5] that helps you understand the people you interact with. Sympathy is a feeling of care and concern *for* a person. Empathy is recognizing and sharing his or her emotions and perspective. Empathy can be summarized as "feeling with." Sympathy can be summarized as "feeling for."

Empathy does not include a psychiatric evaluation or definition, or a peering into the mind or soul of another. Instead, it's a connection in a specific circumstance that provides data for communication, evaluation, decision-making, and leadership. An extreme example is pairs of expert figure skaters, who anticipate each other not only when their routines go well but also when they need to adjust to a misstep.

When empathy is present in a relationship (a pair), both tend to feel safer and more confident because the other person seems like an ally instead of a competitor or antagonist. Notice that this safety is not the product of shared analysis, goals, or values. Instead, it's built on the expectation of a nearly automatic benefit of the doubt. Practice together is powerful, and it also builds the kinds of emotional connection that enables both to perform better together than they would have individually.

How to "Get" Empathy

The brain uses a "system of interconnected brain structures including the amygdala and orbitofrontal cortex to help process emotions, make decisions, control impulses and set goals." These areas of the brain are plastic, that is, they can be changed by more intensive use, just as most brain cells can be.[6] The capacity to develop empathy is available to most people, although it varies in strength.

Empathy involves different experiences with each person. The observational skills can be the same, but the individual's experience will be her own. Here are some cues to begin practicing. Before you start, give yourself some space away from the crush of the day so that you'll be more personally aware of the other person. In each case, focus on one person and pay close attention to cues like these to help answer the question, "What could they be feeling now?"

1. Gaze: Attentive, wandering, looking away.

2. Posture: Leaning toward the speaker, leaning away, slumping.

3. Tone of voice: Animated, neutral, monotone.

4. Questions: Perceptive, frequent, and intense; or commonplace repetitions.

Another way to think about it is to ask yourself, "Is this person interested in me and what I'm doing, or are they just going through the motions?" If you can't tell, your empathy detector is closed. To open it up, check yourself: Are you nervous, trying to push your point of view, looking down on them, feeling superior, or rushing to finish a laborious conversation? This checking yourself is called "countertransference," or observing the ways that you react to another person. Those reactions can be powerful diagnostics for your own skill-building. Unless you are genuinely interested in the other person, you'll miss much of what they offer, let alone have limited ability to team up with or even influence them.

How to Use Empathy

Problem-solving. Problem-solving with another person involves a data triangle: feelings, thoughts, and facts that reside in three areas—your mind, the other person's mind, and external "facts."

For many questions, better data can produce better answers sooner. The diagram can be analyzed in pairs, showing clearly that data from any two is incomplete:

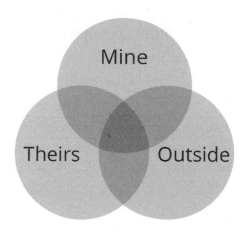

◊   Their data + outside data ignores what I know.

◊   My data + their data ignores outside reality.

◊   My data + outside data ignores what they know.

Empathy tip: When you step into the other's shoes, slip into their head long enough to look out at the world through their eyes. Stay there for fifteen seconds, absorbing what you see. Like most worthwhile endeavors, it takes skill and practice. The payback will amaze you if you work at it. One proven technique was first clarified by Timothy Gallwey in his book *The Inner Game of Tennis*. After prescribing concentration on the seams of a ball to "create time" to hit the ball, he explains how he continues to concentrate in a match. The problem, not unlike life, is that between points there is an explosion of noise in your head: thoughts about the next point, the last point, what needs to be done at home after the match, who is watching, and so forth. His trick is to focus on his breathing between points! The focus is on observing, not controlling your breathing because you don't need to help your lungs perform. As Timothy Gallwey notes, "When the mind is fastened on the rhythm of breathing, it tends to become relaxed and calm. . . . Anxiety is fear about what may happen in the future. . . . But when your attention is on the here and now, the actions which need to be done in the present have their best chance of being accomplished."[7]

Create an environment of higher performance. In addition to common ways of reducing noise—room treatment, white noise, closed-door conference rooms, anti-yelling rules (just made up that last one; who does that?)—empathy between pairs of people can remarkably impact the work environment. And as one of the best restaurant entrepreneurs you've never met says, "It's cheap!"

If you look outside at our world, you'll spot powerful trends that are sneaking under our doors, enveloping all of us who aren't living in a climbing tent on the slope of 22,000-foot-high Mount Aconcagua in the Andes Mountains.

VUCA is a military acronym that, like the Internet, is creeping into our lives. It stands for "volatile, uncertain, complex, and ambiguous," and it sounds like a familiar descriptor of life around us. What's new is its acceleration. Its nose is well into our tents, creating anxiety (fear) about our futures.

One of the fundamentals of dealing with fear espoused by beefy movie heroes is to move right into it. It's a great principle for everyone else but us, especially me when I'm afraid. The power of empathy, of course, is that it can create pairs who will grapple with fear for each other, and drain its power to dilute their best offerings.

Increasing hope and reducing fear. Robert Johansen in his book *Leadership Literacies* paints a compelling picture of our future, leaking now into our present, that is a combination of escalating fear and enhanced hope. The VUCA challenge is to boost hope because VUCA will continue, likely with greater intensity.

Here are three paths to boost hope, in Johansen's view:

Seek clarity instead of certainty. The difference is that clarity is expressed in stories, not rules, which embrace the essential nuances of reality in ways that can satisfy the drive for understanding without providing false insights. In his book *On Being Certain: Believing You Are Right Even When You Are Not,* neuroscientist Robert Burton demonstrates the certainty fallacy: We can feel we're right and be flat wrong. He says, "Certainty and similar states of 'knowing we know' arise out of involuntary brain mechanisms that, like love or anger, function independently of reason."[8]

Explore voluntary fear engagement. Fear is far more debilitating than we realize when looking over our leadership teams. We are trained to hide feelings about it, to act instead as though we're "fine" amid fearsome possibilities. Most of us partition fear-inducing situations away from our everyday lives and give them an as-if reality. For many years, I windsurfed avidly either on the mile-wide Columbia River or in the ocean off Maui. Rational examination would spark fear in either place: The river offered 200-foot-long tugboats and barges with zero ability to turn or stop. The ocean included both sharks and coral, both capable of skin-shredding pain.

I was afraid every time I stepped into the water. The act of stepping into the water was stepping into the fear, reducing it enough for me to function well enough to get back at the end of the trip.

Johansen and others prescribe regularly stepping into the fear by using games as a safe alternative to BASE jumping or swordplay. There are now games that go beyond shoot to kill, involving worldwide teams and visceral competition. Ergo, fear of losing, a healthy step into personal fear. So yes, I prescribe the most intoxicating competitive game that you can tolerate as part of your executive development program. Why not?

Gaming for grit. The book *Grit* by Angela Duckworth paints a research-deep picture of the definition and path to enhanced grit. VUCA demands not only resilience—the ability to recover from a hit—but persistence through diversion and difficulty. There are now games of suitable sophistication to seduce executive leaders into competing intensely over time. The grit required to stay in the game will carry over to the "game" of repeatedly leading into VUCA. VUCA promises to be a succession of trips into a dark room, particularly for leaders, where uncertainty and its relatives strain both leadership and continuity. That leadership persistence is a requirement to continually light the fire of hope. It offers some certainty in the uncertainty of VUCA that will infiltrate our work and home lives. That certainty can frame hopeful efforts, recovery, revision, and renewed vitality, which are the foundation of successful pairs, teams, and organizations.

Empathetic Tradition

How you lead impacts your people, but it also impacts *their* people: their current subordinates, new hires, folks transferred into the department, and the people who they train. Because the sum of daily behaviors of folks around us becomes the environment that we work in, the power of this concept is far beyond occasional kindliness.

The idea of generational transmission of trauma is a suitable model if you replace the word "trauma" with "empathy." The concept goes back as far as the Bible: "The sins of the fathers will be visited upon the sons." Or now, children who are beaten are more likely to beat their children, perpetuating a cycle that can wither generations. Remarkably, however, a significant portion of abused children grow up without a trauma hangover, live healthy lives, and do not pass along their pain. Although part of the trauma transmission mechanism is genetic, much of it is not. Further, therapy and training can mitigate the impact of trauma in the life of the victim, as well as reducing the chance that they will pass on their trauma.

What does this have to do with empathy? If empathy is a way toward authentic connection that steps outside rank and power, then it's worth developing as a human being, as well as a leader. Empathy can be learned, or more correctly, natural inclinations can be reinforced through training and by the example of leaders. Bruce Cazenave, CEO of Nautilus, a successful leader in multiple companies, has a way of being immediately present to nearly everyone. It's a powerful experience to have this man asking a personal question about something that he knows that I value—in my case, my car. His knack is to suggest that he's more interested in what the car means to *me* than in discussing specifications or mechanical high points.

When I asked him in an interview how he came to become such a close student of his people, he described working early in his career for a senior executive at Black & Decker. You guessed it: The Black & Decker guy worked hard to know details about each of his people *and asked about them.* There's your intergenerational transmission model in action.

Empathy toward yourself. Many leaders I know are unconscious masters, unaware of their techniques or their impact on others. The door to self-observation stays open in most of us for brief bursts, often delivered by a spouse, children, or a disgruntled employee, sad to say. Many leaders I've known have an intellectual understanding of their impact, but few develop the visceral connection that empowers human connection and commitment.

When I was president of a midsize manufacturing firm, I hid the car that I loved for fear that it would prejudice employees against me. Yes, hid it—parked where I thought no employee would find it. It was a midlevel BMW, the best that I could afford, and I loved having it and driving it. I misunderstood my impact on my employees, however. Instead of jealousy about my car and anger toward me (which I feared), I was shocked to look up from my desk one day to see the smiling face of our best machinist. He emigrated to the United States with his family when he was young, and still spoke with a Central European accent. He asked, "Where did you get the snow tires? They don't have studs." Clearly, he knew exactly where my car was parked, looked at it enough to see that the snow tires replaced the regular tires, and cared deeply about it, in detail (he's a machinist, so no surprise). I soon learned that most of our workers counted that car as "our car" and were so proud to be associated with it that they "counseled me" whenever there was a bump or a mark on it!

ALLOW FOR CHOICE OF PARTNERS

Some pairs work better than others, and thoughtful pairing can improve results, or at least avoid creating problems. For example, when assigning a team to a project, consider including pairs who have shown that they work well together. This seems obvious, but it may produce a stronger team than one chosen for technical ability or experience alone. Even better, ask for volunteers for a team, and arrange the asking to enable folks to see "who's on the team," so that pairs who work well together can put themselves on the team.

The reverse can also work. A team that doesn't know each other well can be an opportunity for new strong pairs to develop, adding to the potential strength of leadership and project work in the company. It's appealing to think that there's a process for matching pairs, but remind yourself of the mystery of dating and marriage: We're very complex, and simple algorithms probably won't deliver the "click" that strong pairing can. Instead, building a team or a pair for an especially tough project can be a great way for folks to get acquainted—and some strong pairs may emerge because of it!

Most supervision happens in pairs, not in meetings. And supervisors choose a fraction of the folks who report to them (despite their wishes). Over time, supervisors may replace folks who are a bad fit with those who will hopefully be easier to work with, but the questions supervisors face with new relationships almost always include these:

◊ How do I get the person to tell me the straight stuff?

◊ How will they let me help them?

◊ How can we build a relationship that's mostly about each of us bringing what we can to the situation, rather than role-playing or posing, or worse?

Remarkably, building empathy can accelerate development of a relationship that includes all of these, and more. For openers, your empathetic techniques will fail if they're for manipulation or a hidden objective. Even more important, if your goal serves you instead of the company or them, you'll fail in a fog of suspicion. Instead, start by asking for help—genuine help about a real problem that's a challenge for you. If you fold in respect for the other person's skills and ignore their rank in the company, you're off to a good start.

A client, a senior officer in a major corporation, found himself tagged with a company initiative that required tools he didn't have. The corporate vice president of legal and human resources had a budget and links to outside experts, but our hero's relationship with the VP was mixed up with differences in rank and power. When he sat down in the VP's office as a guy asking for help, with nothing to negotiate, he found a man pleased to offer help who confided some of his own fears about the task in front of them. He moved from a suspicious distance to a comfortable pairing built on mutual empathy!

Linking Pairs

Linking pairs almost always delivers better results if part of the preparation includes working with each person individually first to clarify their interest and concerns in the proposed pairing. This exercise can be dramatically powered up by using the kindness trio technique, outlined below.[9]

Use the same techniques with an individual and when joining a pair: First, identify a key person or a pair to lead the effort. Next, set a goal such as increased focus, higher output, fewer errors, and so forth in agreement with the person or pair. Then shift to the kindness trio technique:

Think about a characteristic of this person that you appreciate. Look for something that creates some feelings in you or at least a sense of respect. Use that insight as a doorway to working kindly with the person.

Put down your shield. This is no commune from California; it's an approach borrowed from skilled hostage negotiators. You may think that you and your people are fundamentally different from folks who take hostages, but there is little difference in much of your psychological makeup. So, take advantage of these insights.

Gather data about what's going on in that person's mind (empathy). Empathy is your recognition that the other person's mind is involved and has information that can help you both. It is your job to learn this information and to make it easy for the other person to share. (Warning: If you try to use this to take advantage of the other person, they'll see it and you risk losing their trust for a long, long time.)

Treat that person with deference. Not just respect, but deference. Skip the power politics. Face the fact that this person has something that you want: their skill, attention, motivation, and so forth. Deference means treating them as someone who has power, respect, and a strong place in the world, and you are happy to get to work with them. Your deference will enable the next gentle exploration:

◊ What are they afraid of losing? What's on the table in this discussion for them, especially things they value that they might be afraid they'd lose?

Slow down, inquire for data. You're looking for information, not for an advantage.

◊ When you see what they fear losing, say it out loud: "It seems like there's more going in than meets the eye here for you. Is that true?"

◊ Listen closely.

◊ The point of this approach is to accept the delightful truth that most people have way more to offer than you allow them to provide. The leadership task is to provide two contrasting elements: focus and depth.

You have two primary tasks here:

◊ Provide a frame for the work. This frame is like a hallway leading to a room. The room is the goal, or what will it look like when we get there; the hallway is the boundary of where to look and what to ask. Framing must be a two-way conversation, both to assure mutual understanding and to find the best possible objective.

◊ Provide an empathic invitation for them to participate. "Empathic" means that it feels safe to them, freeing them to offer what they have straight up.

When this approach is applied, the immediate effect is often wonder: wonder at the burst of ideas, wonder at their quality, wonder at the speed of movement. It's invigorating enough to convert unfamiliar pairs into folks who can't wait to work together again.

Chapter 3

Leadership Express

This chapter will uncover the hidden secret of high-performance organizations. It is what their people do about the operating data that surrounds them, including daily and weekly measures. It blows away the myth that fully formed dashboards are the power station for success. Instead, managing people carefully with a detailed guidance system can yield amazing results.

WHY YOU NEED TWO SETS OF BOOKS

Successful leadership requires the split vision of Janus, the Roman god of beginnings and endings, whose two faces look to the future and the past. This simple principle may have the highest impact of anything in this book. It's a bit like a hummingbird: Look closely or you'll miss it. Business investors (including lenders and owners) use the same information as leaders but use it differently. Corollary: Measuring is not the same as leading, financial analysts to the contrary notwithstanding. Investors look back like physicians, answering the question, "How are we doing?" to measure health and forecast future outcomes from a flood of data in monthly or quarterly chunks. Their focus is risk, preventing a decline from planned outcomes ("normal").

With all this complexity, how can data help a leader? The idea is to use the data in the right "time zone." Monthly financials, for a leader, are useful only in three areas:

◊ Marking the limits that capital requires. Loan covenants and owner rates of return on capital are the fences that mark the limits of the playing field. Go past them at your peril.

◊ Tracking subtle change in the business model. Over time, profitability will either slide or grow. Sliding requires action to preserve cash; growth offers an opportunity to invest for further success (bonuses, hiring, equipment) or additional payout to owners.

◊ Maintaining adequate cash. Cash consumers such as inventory, slow receivables, or expenses can be checked monthly, like blood pressure, to spot needed correctives.

By now you notice that these are all "external" measures, lurking outside the flow of the business to provide warning lights calling for adjustment. The problem is that they say little about the business itself. Just as you wouldn't drive by the warning lights on your dash, you risk your business if you lead it based upon the data in your monthly financials. It really is too little and way too late because months of data are needed to reveal a trend that matters. Here's an example of how it looks:

January	February	March	April
Business actions	Accounting reports prepared	Results reported, actions planned	Actions implemented

Yes, it's April before powerful reactions to January are implemented! Four months—one third of your fiscal year. That four-month lag never catches up and is a problem for all but firms with no growth and no change. So, what's a leader to do?

> *People who enjoy meetings should not be in charge of anything.*
>
> *—Thomas Sowell[3]*

Monday Dilemma

Every Monday morning, millions of workers enter their workplaces and decide what to do next. A frightening thought. The most important issue is not what they do but how they choose what to do. The noise of competing inbox requests, amplified by personal preference and cultural imperatives, is a powerful diversion from any plan or goal. That noise is as permanent as the light in the room, and as invisible.

Most folks want to do the right thing, but the noise obscures that "right thing" much of the time. One way to cut through the noise is to provide some structure to the minutes, days, and weeks. The outcome of a basketball game builds upon what happens in the minutes of the game. It's not about preparation, time-outs with the coach and chalkboard, and certainly not what the scoreboard or time clock says. It uses all these, but it's about what's done minute by minute in the game. The coach's job is to fill each minute with the right actions by his team. Your business is the same. How can you guide what happens minute by minute?

Leaders look forward, answering the question, "What can we do now?" A three-dimensional view explains some of the complexity of leadership. Not only does a leader look back and forward, but she also looks through multiple time dimensions in her job to plot a path and keep her organization on it. Leaders and their teams plan for years, measure in months, and work in minutes. Beyond the cliché about driving while looking in the rearview mirror, the leadership question really is, "What is useful in the pile of data in front of us?

Goal alignment is wrongly praised as the essential solution to this problem, as though an organization were static, like the linkage of engine/transmission/drive shaft/differential/axle/wheels in a car. Each part in a car moves, but it is restricted by its connections. Business has no such built-in restrictions, beyond individual ethics and culture. Alignment's false promise is that once attained, constructive linkage will guide the business to success.

Instead, the secret to alignment is to reverse directions: imagine the wheels telling the engine what to do! This is not a feeble plea for bottoms-up leadership, that somehow "the people know." They do, in their limited perspectives, but self-directed teams failed by the end of the last century in a mix of power squabbles and deluded aim.

Instead of standardized work, provide a structure to answer workers' questions:

◊   What is our goal?

◊   How are we doing?

◊   How am I doing?

◊   What needs doing?

And then leave space for them to do what's needed, providing help when necessary. The foundation of the system is to change from prescribing work in detail to reporting progress against a target that most employees want to reach.

The structure is a fabric that frames and reports results in minutes, days, and weeks, and builds in the actions needed next. In fabric-talk, it's the warp. The weft (cross-threads) of your fabric are the review sessions (RAM) that process the data and extract next actions in the sparest and clearest way. Both the data and the discussion require a surgeon's clarity and a coach's drive for action.

This system demands a fundamental shift from measuring success in months and quarters to measuring success in weeks. The core question becomes, "What will it take to make the week?" The principle is: Make the day; make the week; make the month. Repeat.

The numbers by themselves won't sustain excellence, regardless of the strength of the team. What sustains excellence is personal drive—the emotional push that wants to hit the target. What's the formula for that emotional push? It's KPIs + RAM = EP (emotional push).

You Need Metrics to Tell How Fast You're Going

Metrics, or KPIs, are proudly brandished by most leaders. In my experience few leaders use them to guide the work of their people, missing the remarkable power of KPIs. There are three problems that block most of them:

1. Measuring the wrong things in the wrong time periods.

2. Believing that numbers alone will motivate people.

3. Not quickly sharing for broad understanding.

Let's take a closer look at each of these.

Measuring the Wrong Things: Dashboard Dilemma

Picture the dashboard—of an airliner, perhaps? There is a dial or a light for just about everything on the plane except ordering a martini. Problem is, they are designed

mostly to highlight problems, not to improve performance. For your business, that means reinforcing business as usual, tyranny by inbox, reaction to problems.
There's little in there for improvement, raising the bar,
or keeping up with competitors, let alone getting ahead
of them. Not good, in a world whirling with change.

If you ask CEOs, as I have, most will tell you that
their dashboard contains fifteen to twenty-five numbers. Most can't recall much beyond sales. Dashboards
can be elaborate security blankets (Linus would love
them) full of "just in case" numbers. They are dutifully calculated each month, and occasionally are the subject
of a meeting. They are too many to remember, mostly
provide needless analysis of monthly financials, and
provide limited direction about what to do next (beyond "we need more cash").

When fans enter a baseball park or basketball game
(even in grade school), they reflexively check the scoreboard before sitting down. Don't you? This proves two
things about most folks:

1. They want to know the score.

2. They want to understand the score.

Even though these are not the same (go back and
read them again), KPI-builders across the country con-
flate the two, if more is better. That's not how scoreboards are designed, and not how people think. Proof:
Recall your scoreboard—the score is in huge numbers,
hard to miss. The analysis (number of team fouls, number of timeouts remaining, etc.) is in smaller numbers,

sometimes not on all sides of the scoreboard, and so forth. Here's your test question: If you entered the gym knowing that you had to leave in sixty seconds because your car just burst into flames, what numbers would you want to see? If you chose number of fouls, see me after class. Of course not! It's the score!

If KPIs are scoreboards, shouldn't they be arranged to show the score first and the analysis second (in emphasis, size, noise, etc.)?

Believing that Numbers Alone Will Motivate People

Numbers alone aren't motivating at all, and more numbers don't deliver a power boost. If the point of KPIs is to guide the folks doing the work, instead of helping the CFO glow with pride, shouldn't the folks know what they mean? How will they know what the numbers mean, or what's good, unless there's a comparison with something? Doubt it? How many scoreboards have you seen where there is only one score (your team, let's say), so there's no way to tell who's ahead? The number occasionally means something (highest-scoring game, etc.), but usually it's the comparison that packs the punch.

For a worker to be moved by a KPI, these things are required:

1. Workers understand the meaning.

2. Workers can compare the current number to something (yesterday, goal).

3. Workers can keep the number in their heads.
   Yes! Surprise! It's the same as fans talking about a

game over a beer. They remember the score, and some of the plays that made it happen.

Mark Donegan, CEO of Precision CastParts ($500 million maker of specialty castings for airplane engines), is notorious for visits to company manufacturing sites. He'll invariably ask a machine operator, "What were our numbers yesterday?" The expectation is that any worker may be asked, and every worker knows yesterday's numbers, usually for the company and his unit. Workers who don't know their numbers give their supervisors the gift of Donegan's wrath. Isn't this the same as a basketball player or football player checking the scoreboard and the time clock? You're in the game or you're not. If you're in, the passion to do well explodes from the KPIs to the folks doing the work in each minute of the day.

Simple point: If you limit your KPIs to three numbers, your people can know them and take their game up a notch. What's at play is emotion, even more than rational numbers.

It's so simple that we miss it. Real numbers can keep us closer to reality and help us avoid making the next decision based upon our deeply held beliefs. In his book *Thinking, Fast and Slow,* Daniel Kahneman pictures the repertory of skilled responses that all of us build up over time. We access those responses quickly and automatically to answer a problem facing us. This works well so often that most of us have a lousy system of spotting an error when we make a judgment. Kahneman: "We would all like to have a warning bell that rings loudly whenever we are about to make a serious error, but no such bell is available."[1] So much is at stake at each stage of action in the business that our bias toward good news pulls us away from the problems that need rapid attention, and blinds us toward seeing news that's better than we expect.

Here are some guidelines to put punch in your KPIs:

1. Design each to deliver maximum impact on profitability and customer satisfaction. Test your KPI: If this number improves, will your financials and customer satisfaction improve? If there's no clear link, go back and refine your KPI.

2. Tie each number to a specific item on the monthly financials or customer satisfaction.

3. Choose carefully and narrowly.

4. Find a single measure that captures performance in many areas.

5. Define precisely and publicly, in writing.

6. Work through the definitions with the folks who will use them.

7. Never use more than three measures.

8. Measure and report daily.

9. Roll up into weeks and months.

10. Present the goal and performance in each report.

11. Put these in front of every employee every day. This requires sharing bad and good news, which will boost morale remarkably.

At a manufacturing firm where I worked, we used that framework to design new KPIs. We tested them in several stages to be sure that they were accurate and consistently reported what we thought they were reporting. We presented them publicly in a three-month test to start to teach people how to use them and how to spot inconsistencies or sloppy meaning. The first full year we were live, operating profit jumped millions of dollars over the prior year. The result was so big that I didn't believe it, and I confronted the CFO about the reports. He said he'd already checked and rechecked and stood by his numbers.

Not Sharing Quickly for Broad Understanding

Without an umbilical to the people in the business, measures are decoration. KPI power comes from what people do about them. Harness this power by shoving essential KPIs in front of every employee every day. Forget about competition, security, union leverage, or any other laziness masquerading as protection for the business. If you paint your numbers on the side of your building, your competitor won't know what to do with them. If your key leaders ignore your bright new KPIs, set up company computers so when they boot up in the morning, the first thing they show is the latest KPIs. Your IT team will try to avoid it, but when it's done, your people will love it! Everyone wants to know "how we're doing."

How to Speed Up by Slowing Down

The word on meetings is mixed but mostly negative. In the manufacturing firm mentioned previously (the one in which profit improved "millions"), we used ten-minute daily meetings for production team leads to review yesterday's KPIs. The production manager violently objected (no fighting or swearing, but about every other kind of objection). His view was that workers should be on the production floor operating their machines or the company was wasting time and the labor dollars to pay them ("I want to see those machines going up and down every minute!"). He calculated the cost per minute for the meetings to prove what a bad idea they were. His experience was that if he wasn't watching his workers, they'd slow down, make mistakes, and so forth. After we began to get the results mentioned above, I asked him if he was ready to cancel the meetings. He looked at me like I'd lost my mind: "Absolutely not!"

The system that delivered those results is far more than the numbers. Let's look at how we took the time to build that system and got added profit built on bounding energy and pride among the folks in the company. We spent time with all departments to choose the three most powerful KPIs to measure. "Powerful" meant influence on financial and customer results. The three we chose:

1. Shipment units and dollars.

2. Quality.

3. Efficiency.

Crucial point: We measured at the shipping door, just before product left us for our customers. Earlier measures can be easier to make, but actions or accidents later in the process can change the actual results. After all, we bill our customers and book our shipments when they go out the door, not earlier. Remarkably, the easiest place to grab the numbers is often at the "back door" of your company. The focus can be restricted to counting, instead of other production activity.

All businesses are production businesses. There are customers, marketing, selling, orders, processes to prepare product for delivery to customers, actual delivery, billing, receipt of payment, and so forth. Some of the best techniques for assuring quality and efficiency have come out of the production world. Your product and your company are special and unique, but there's lots to learn from others.

To come up with the measures, we talked through each measure in small groups involving every employee. We worked through the definitions to come up with something that everyone could understand and support and showed examples of how they were calculated. No measure is immediately obvious to all employees, despite what you think. Here are examples:

Shipments. Are they counted when they arrive on the shipping dock, when they are palletized and ready to ship, when they are loaded on the truck, or when the truck departs?

Quality. Do you wait for customer complaints, as we did in the trash-hauling business? (Every customer whose

trash wasn't picked up on pickup day will call. *Every.*
One. Don't you?) In this rare case, we had nearly 100
percent information about the quality of our service because customers would immediately let us know about
quality problems. If your customers won't call as reliably as trash customers, how can you know how you're
doing? Start by insisting on a measure, and ask your
customer-facing people what should be tracked. Quality measures in the production process are necessary
for production control, but they are seldom enough for
this metric. Here are some techniques to figure your
quality KPI:

◊   As product is packed, check either all of it or
    a representative sample. Your quality team can
    provide a sampling framework for the reliability
    you seek.

◊   Track missed appointments.

◊   Wait for customer calls.

◊   Track customer complaints in your service center.

◊   Ask your salespeople to report every case of cus-
    tomer dissatisfaction.

Efficiency. This can be a measure of labor efficiency
(units per labor hour or dollar) or of on-time shipment (or
delivery). The on-time measure, if tracked accurately, can
be a devastatingly correct measure of how well customers are served and how efficiently resources are used.

The Blinding Speed of Leverage

Here is where the pieces of your leadership express system combine to provide leverage for remarkable results. You are building the measures-targets-adjustment (MTA) system described below, offering advanced guidance for your business. All your measures amount to little unless they help adjust the direction of the business. An unvoiced cliché is that good "planning" will frame the company's direction and keep it on the right heading. Not true. Especially not true when the direction and adjustments remain in the head of the leader.

At a printing company where I worked, the CEO doubted the benefit of a budget because "we know what we're doing." Beneath that was a controlling top-down leadership that no longer kept up with the company's growth. When Scott, the production manager, switched from telling his managers what to do to defining the problems for them to solve, cost reduction delivered a one-third increase in annual earnings—in two months! (Yes, he used a version of MTA.)

You can do even more than Scott did. Apply a full MTA to your organization. Think of MTA as an exoskeleton for your business and its people. It's like the fences and rules that make a baseball game a competition instead of a free-for-all. Once in place, understood, and employed, you'll see surprising talent and performance emerge with more enthusiasm and less effort by you and your leaders.

MTA: Measures + Targets + Adjustment = Results that Will Surprise You

Measures. Define performance measures that are precisely machined to their purpose. Commonly divided between financial measures and operating measures, the guiding principle is that the shorter-term operating measures (days, weeks, months) drive financial results (month, quarter, year). The clearer that linkage, the more effective both data sets are.

Here are their definitions:

MEASURE	FREQUENCY
Financial reports with analysis (P&L, balance sheet, cash flow)	Monthly, quarterly, annually
Budgets mimicking P&L, cash flow	Monthly, quarterly, annually
KPIs	Daily, weekly

Targets (goals). Goals put power into measures. Carefully defined measures enable targets that can be believable enough to excite employees to high performance, properly used. Define the measures before the targets so that confidence in the measures can translate to commitment to believable goals. If your people don't understand or believe the measures, the goals will sit unused on the desk. The most powerful targets are daily or weekly, so folks can see how they did "yesterday" and adjust quickly.

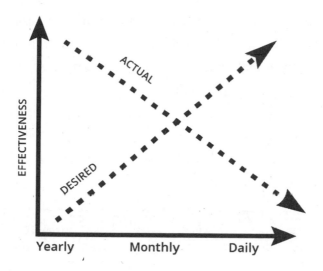

Adjustments. This is where your tools guide people to impact results. Adjustments to return to the path (targets) of success are vital, challenging to maintain, and wonderfully rewarding as they become embedded as "how we do things here." The point of MTA is the adjustment phase.

People are an organization's leverage, for good or ill. At all three levels of organization—management team, middle management, and team leads—people's leverage can be stunning if they are properly trained and guided to use your MTA. Sadly, too many focus on the measures and targets instead of vital adjustment review sessions that bring everyone into the game.

A physical therapy organization with multiple clinics faced dramatic cuts in reimbursement because of changes in insurance law. Key results posted weekly in each clinic sparked a fulcrum meeting, the output of which was simply the organization's focus for the week. Their work was a main reason that the organization sold for three times the expected value to a sophisticated national chain that wanted to use their systems in their hundred-plus clinics.

After you've built measures and targets, bring results alive in your adjustment system, called review and modify (RAM) sessions. The best leaders organize these into two parts: frame and game.

Level	Frequency	Length
One-on-One	Weekly	30 minutes
Team and lead	Daily	10 minutes
Department manager and leads	Daily	10 minutes
Management team	Weekly	10 minutes
All hands	Quarterly	60–90 minutes

In basketball, the frame is the floor with out-of-bounds lines, basket, free-throw line, and the rules that define them. Your computer requires protocols and sequences to deliver the results that you want. Your fulcrum session frame can do the same. It's a supercharger for great results. When there's no frame, there's no game, no results, no fun, and no motivation.

Here's your basic RAM session frame. Like the basketball court, it's the same for every game (meeting):

◊ Include leader and direct reports only. Other levels cripple discussion.

◊ Attend religiously. Tell employees they'll be there unless they're on vacation, sick, or dead.

◊ Have a fixed list of group members. Guests join to present or observe (no questions).

◊ No substitutes.

◊ Meet on the same day, same time.

◊ Meet in same place, with agenda, whiteboard, and clock.

◊ Hard start time; expect all to be in the room five minutes early.

◊ Hard stop time.

◊ Rotating timekeeper to stay on agenda time.

◊ Same length of meeting each time.

◊ For ten-minute meetings, all stand. If longer, then sit around a table.

◊ Adapt meeting frequency, time, and agenda for the levels in your company.

◊ Use the same agenda in every meeting of the same type. (See examples.)

Sample Agenda
Daily Stand-up Meeting Team and Lead

◊ Yesterday's results

◊ People:

  » Absent

  » Need help/Give help

  » Overtime

◊ Equipment problems

◊ Building problems

◊ Today's tough jobs

◊ Roadblocks

◊ Safety

Sample Agenda:
Management Team Meeting

◊ 1:25: All here

◊ 1:30: My 1–3 priorities for this week: Name in a minute; go around the table

◊ 1:40: Results for week and month:

  » Metrics

  » Monthly financials (Week 3 only)

◊ 2:00: Sales update (Week 4 only)

◊ 2:10: Past action list update

◊ 2:20: New issues

» Solve in three minutes, or post to action list, parking lot, or drop)

◊   2:45: Done

Output:

◊   Surface issues that organization isn't solving, and triage:

» Solve in three minutes, action list, parking lot, drop

◊   Action list: What, who, when; in Excel; to all by end of meeting day

Sample Agenda:
One-on-One Meeting

1. Progress on last week's top three
2. Your action items from management team
3. Progress toward your goals
4. Progress on financial and operating metrics
5. Major issues now
6. Next week's top three

For each item:

◊   What's working well?

◊   What are roadblocks now?

◊   How can I help?

Initiatives. Review of initiatives works best with different data than operating results versus targets. Instead, use two layers of information: status and problems.

Consider the approach that Alan Mulally used as a foundation to turn around Ford Motor Company from 2006 through 2009:

Soon after joining Ford, CEO Alan Mulally initiated priority rankings in his mandatory weekly BPR (business plan review) meetings, using these colors:

Red—Not on plan, no strategy to get on plan

Yellow—Not on plan but has a strategy to get on plan

Green—On plan and all is good

The company then was losing $18,000,000, and yet everyone's priorities showed "Green." Alan: "I guess our plan must be to lose billions of dollars!"

Weeks passed. Finally, somebody said, "Red—not on plan, no strategy to get there." Alan stood up and applauded. He said, "You know you're not on plan and you don't know how to get there. It's okay. Thank you for having the courage to say that."

Then Alan said, "Neither of us knows how to get on plan, and that's okay. Why don't we just find people that know the answer?"[4]

The Game

Picture the room with six or eight folks who are itching to see how they did, so they can go out doing even better. The emotional feel of the room is at least as critical as the data, and no one has a monopoly on the will to do better.

This approach brings data into the room with folks who can use it immediately. The outcome of RAM meetings is specific actions—framed who, what, and when. Communication, both down and up, are data for use in defining action. Broadly theoretical or philosophic communication has its place, but including it in these meetings risks hopelessly hiding needed actions.

Meetings are primarily about the people in the room and what they choose to do. Once the data is in their laps, their leader's skill determines the power to get the right things done.

Let's shift to leader behavior because it's the other accelerant (after data). Each of these principles can power the astonishing results.

Frame the time in the room as a treasure hunt open to all. The leader has no monopoly on truth. Instead, his job is to help every member dive into the pool of data, bring back possible actions, and put his shoulder behind every action the group chooses. Let me say this another way: The leader's job is to help every member in the room. It's not to solve problems. Few actions corrupt commitment and motivation faster than a leader who "knows the answer." As Alan Mulally said, "For the great achiever, it's all about me. And for the great leader it's all about them."[5]

The leader's job in the room:

◊   Listen closely.

◊   Ask penetrating questions about the data.

◊ Support each person: "It seems that you have some ideas in mind."

◊ Model curiosity before judgement: "Why is that? What would it mean?"

◊ Delay the drive to decide, just a bit, substituting curiosity.

◊ Pace the discussion to balance inquiry with action steps.

◊ Pull for action out loud when it's time to shift to action from exploration.

◊ Insist on intended actions enthusiastically supported as the meeting's result.

◊ Insist on following the agenda.

◊ Find laughter.

◊ Ensure communication with folks not in the room, who likely do the work.

Rate your performance. You and the team should rate you as leader on the items above.

Grade each item:

10 = excellent

7 = satisfactory

5 = needs improvement

Total your scores and pay attention to the tens as well as the fives.

Every day, your leaders and your people are doing *something*. Your challenge is to help them more and more to do the things that impact the results that the company and its customers want. It's a live thing, like a racehorse, and like a horse it can be managed for better outcomes.

Chapter 4

The Architecture of the Business

When I worked at a major food retailer in Chicago, I was part of a cross-functional team that designed new stores. When I objected to small back rooms in a store, I heard advice for the ages: Set conditions that help people do the right thing. In this store's back rooms, that meant the limited space would drive excellence in stocking shelves and ordering, to prevent the out-of-stock situations that drive customers away.

It elegantly reversed the instinct that more inventory would reduce out-of-stocks. And it worked to simplify the management job because there was little back-room stock to be counted, repositioned, dragged, and dragged again out to the store aisle to be put on the shelf. It was "flow" before "lean" was a thing: unloaded from the truck through the back room to the store shelves, with empty spots on shelves immediately spotlighting out-of-stocks.

The Limits of Hands-On Leadership

As soon as a company has more than ten employees, daily leadership tasks outstrip any hands-on leader. A glaring oxymoron, hands-on is a substitute for leadership, not a condition for success. The exception is the leader of a work team of eight to twelve workers doing "production" work, which ranges from entering accounting data to ordering materials to working in a call center. A working leader can be effective if his leadership responsibilities are training, organizing the day's work, and reporting discipline or performance issues to his supervisor.

Let's shoot the myth of omniscient leadership now. Strength is not wisdom. Leadership is not like quarterbacking a football game, where the team waits for the next guidance to react for thirty seconds. The player-coach is an anachronism in sports and business because almost no one can do the work and lead the work at the same time. The business game never stops, and effective leaders construct fences and cues to nudge toward success and get around obstacles.

Let's look at nudges and cues as fences:

Focus relentlessly on results. The leader's first job is to describe what success looks like. These descriptions, as numbers, need to be so simple and quick that line workers get them instantly. The essential here is to look past the person to the results first. If they are good, move on. If not, rapidly dig in to understand what might improve things.

Set hard frameworks like bowling alley gutters that guide desired processes. These frames live in work processes, or "how we do things here." The trick is systems that are simple enough to learn, operate, and maintain. Complexity should be built into the system but removed from the operator, using technology tools such as macros. Pay as much attention to checkpoints as to simplicity in operation so that errors can be spotted quickly by operators and corrected. Supervisor audits can then focus on output speed and accuracy, relying on operator skill to make needed adjustments.

Separate process audits between operators and supervisors. Operators should look for at least one process improvement to be installed every week, as part of their job. Supervisors can then selectively audit outputs, focusing on problem systems for correction.

Define positions before filling them with people. The collection of positions, called structure, are like the store's back room. If they are right, selecting and training people to do the work is doable. Part of every annual business review should be adjusting job structures to master the coming year's challenges.

Clarify what's in employees' heads. Leaders' jobs include learning what needs to be done for success and providing effective tools to move those ideas from their heads to the heads of the people who will do the work. What matters is what workers know and believe. If only the leaders know, their people will not necessarily do the right things at the right time.

Refine the problem before acting. More people can solve a problem than can define it because we reward solutions more than questions. Great leaders, therefore, are superb questioners and problem definers. In reverse, without crystal clear problems our natural bent toward solutions will pull us to solve the wrong question. That wastes time, money, and competitive advantage.

Reward simplicity. Complexity is the enemy of excellence, often hiding a better way in the blur of misunderstanding. Complexity often will melt in the face of simple questions asked often, such as, "Why are we doing this?" and What would it take to make it simpler?"

A trash hauling company is like a reverse manufacturing operation spread out over miles. The main costs are trucks and drivers, so route efficiency impacts service, quality, and profit. Here's the frame that we set up when I worked with them: The drivers wanted to go home when they finished their routes, instead of working to the end of their shift. The owner required them to return to headquarters and work there until their shift ended to limit accidents, injuries, and customer complaints about being missed or trash spilled, which were more likely (he thought) if drivers hurried to finish earlier.

We set up three frames to track accidents, injuries, and customer complaints publicly every day. After working out the kinks in reporting, we offered modest cash bonuses for months or quarters with no accidents, injuries, or complaints. We soon began paying those bonuses, and the benefits to the company were improved customer service, lower worker's compensation insurance cost, fewer lost-time accidents, and improved morale because drivers could leave work when they finished. Remarkably, net worth rose 20 percent because honest rerouting allowed us to avoid buying another truck to haul items newly required by the cities we served.

Hunt treasure instead of floating in entropy. Entropy is the tendency of all systems (and people) to slide toward average and easy. The daily default can be just emptying your inbox, answering questions from others, and solving the problems that present themselves. If this is your menu as a leader, you're in the grip of entropy, and your future likely will disappoint. It's not just that if you're not getting better, you're sliding backward. It's that your organization is on an accelerating path to the ugly awakening that things are bad and getting worse. Instead, create a treasure map, and bring alive a picture of the treasure to be found. The treasure will be in the building and creating, not just the money and security. To get started, however, picture a future state, and specifically describe it with pictures, numbers, and details.

> *The greatest wisdom not applied to action and behavior is meaningless data.*
>
> —*Peter Drucker*[1]

The People Connection

The people connection is linking real folks with the principles above, after you've made your initial explanation. Here is a starter list of ideas to do that:

Shift from the noise of entropy to simplification and listening. When your people are working within the frames that you and they have created, and they are fighting entropy at the same time, go see them. In person. Go see any employee who doesn't report directly to you. Schedule a weekly hour in your calendar to go see people. Don't follow any pattern. Instead, pick a person and put yourself on their level, literally. If they are standing, stand. If they are sitting, sit. Face them, look at their face, and ask questions like these:

◊   What's on your mind?

◊   How are you doing?

◊   What keeps you from doing your job?

◊   What would you like to change?

After each question, pause and wait for them. Smile. Relax. You're with folks who are rooting for you to help them, regardless of the expression on their face. You represent hope and support when you're there in person. Listen, nod, smile. Then ask, "And what else?"

Thank them. Make no promises because your trip is for you to learn, not for you to give orders to them to change. Listen a lot, act a little (likely the reverse of your impulses). Your knowledge of "how things really are" will inform an upcoming decision.

Be a consulted leader. The power of the consulted leader approach[2] is knowing the details of your people as well as your business. It requires replacing answers with close connection with each of your people, giving them the responsibility and space to find good answers themselves. The power that can be unleashed is beyond your imagination. How many of these can you answer yes to?

1. Understand what's happening with each of your key people most of the time.

2. Frame their job to match their capacity.

3. Frame their responsibilities to match the pace they need to maintain, not the pace you want them to maintain.

4. Connect with people as you walk around. (It's the connection, not just the walk.)

5. Learn the people, not just the work.

6. Make time for people immediately when they ask for help.

7. Lead by questioning, not by providing answers.

8. Listen closely and check that you heard what they meant.

9. Usually craft a second question to clarify critical details.

10. Make every answer part of the other person's body of work instead of yours.

11. Establish trust by offering credibility, close listening, adding value, and helpful thought.

12. Desire to be the first person that people want to talk with.

13. Educate change with the "why"; don't dictate it.

14. Use small moments, when questions pop up without time for preparation, to demonstrate being a consulted leader.

15. Manage diversions, bad or good, to keep work aligned with goals.

Your "yes" answers start you on a road to enhanced leadership, measured by the performance of your people.

Replace answers with questions. It takes repeated conscious effort to hold back your answer to the problem and shift to questions. Questions usually get you better answers with higher commitment, which is preferable to directing the answer and getting compliance.

Here's a starter list:

◊   Why?

◊   What if we didn't?

◊   What is the benefit?

◊   Why do you think that?

The leader should jump in with her insight when it's potentially high return, not obvious, or will need rapid vetting for success.

THE ENTRANCE IS NOT THE EXIT

A favorite story of my mentor Alan Weiss is the planning session with the major accomplishment of moving the content from the premeeting chart to the postmeeting chart unscathed! How often have you worked through a discussion with others to find progress slipping through your fingers like water, leaving only a moist residue? Our reward is limited to pleasure in the discussion, a feeling that we've "worked it," and a pleasant diversion from the thorny issue that needs attention. Outside the room this seems unlikely and obvious, but it's a common reason that work is unfulfilling and organizations seem to be wandering noisily through their days, accomplishing less than hoped.

The Power of Type 5 Meetings

These are the meetings that no one talks about, everyone wants to avoid, and are frequently sold as "retreats"—a weekend at an appealing resort. Sometimes called "long-term strategic planning meetings" (redundant oxymoron), they are none of the above, despite their critical role in aiming the investment and execution of most businesses. So let's give these the payoff that makes them essential. Here's how:

The reason to do it is to recruit the power of a target, even if it's three years into the future. A well-crafted target can aim daily activity, provide a reference for annual and quarterly goals, and enable course correction without the heavy hand of senior leadership. It does the job that a mission statement is supposed to do, but seldom does: invite employees to work together toward a future that they want to bring to life.

Why three years? It's far enough into the future to risk bigger steps; it allows room for adjustment over time; and it can frame critical investment that can't pay back in twelve months. (Five years is fantasy, and such planning sessions produce little else.)

In the meeting, we define our strategy and our tactics using today's descriptors. It's really two meetings:

Strategy grid meeting. What do we want to look like in thirty-six months? Meeting output: A picture in data-set form that brings to life a thirty-six-month target. We'll call it a "grid"—a combination of financial measures and key product/services that powerfully appeal to our target customers. This can literally be an array of numbers, products, and customer types. Its presentation matters less than its simplicity and understandability. Here are examples of common categories of information used to paint this thirty-six-month picture:

◊ Sales, gross margin, pretax profit, earnings before interest and taxes (EBIT).

◊ Number and types of core customers, current and growth targets.

◊ Key products: core profit drivers, core revenue drivers, core growth products and channels.

ITEM	FIRST QUARTER	TOTAL YEAR	36-MONTH GRID
Sales ($000)	10,000	35,000	105,000
Gross margin (%)	30	31	31.5
# of customers, new:	10	45	150
# of customers, existing:	100	125	300

Spend more effort to define the categories than to fill in the numbers. The way you define the categories, like a meal on a smorgasbord table, will define your options. After you've developed the categories, cut their number in half, and fight about their definition in your leadership group so you'll all know what you've signed up for. There's a reason a bulldozer blade has a finite width.

Note to serious players: At this stage, the picture is being painted. The next stage will spell out actions needed in each category to meet the plan. Wait for the picture before you race down the path.

Annual plan (tactics). What specific actions in the next twelve months will move your total company toward each item in your thirty-six-month strategy grid? Meeting output: a list of actions to move toward your annual targets for next year and the quarterly actions to accomplish the year. Frame first for total company, and then challenge each department team to name what they'll do in the coming year, and then quarter by quarter to move toward each company goal.

The power in the process is the quarterly department actions and outcomes. As one wag said, "the company" is a group of people. It's not a thing by itself, so its future depends on what its people do. The sharper and briefer the plan, the more likely success will be. For crisp power, schedule each department head to present an outline of his annual plan to the executive team. Allow fifteen minutes for each, including presentation and discussion. After each group presentation, ask what the toughest goal will be to reach and why. That frames the first progress review question in coming weeks.

Use the rule of three to enhance recall and interest because it's the smallest group of words that creates a pattern. Wherever possible, stop at three goals, examples, paths to execution, and so forth. The point of all this, after all, is to craft targets that live in most employees' minds most days, and influence what they choose to do. Complexity drowns the brain, it seems.

What about a budget? Yes, you'll need one. It's like a map of your journey. It's a reference to show you where things are fine and where they need work. It's not a plan or a strategy, just as a map is not the trip. It should cover monthly results for your coming year, with an earnings statement comparing actual results to budget (and sometimes) last year's results. Used properly, it can help spot areas that need action to return to the path of your plan.

Where does the grist for next year's plans come from? Preparation for the plans (three-year, one-year) and budget can be scheduled for the three months before the grid update meeting, which kicks off the next year's plan. Preparations work best in this sequence:

1. Departments work out the top three opportunities and obstacles (O&O) in their area, looking at the current grid and outside at customers. A word about SWOT, the beloved but impotent exercise reviewing strengths, weaknesses, opportunities, and threats: It takes too long and produces thin gruel at best, so skip it. However, O&O can be put on steroids in a separate session by a department devoted to finding opportunities at the edge of possible. Starting rules include ignoring costs, prior practice, competition, and the rest. Instead, imagine projecting company competence to new customers and adding new products or services. That template should produce at least one power concept that can be built into another foundation of company success. It is fair to copy other companies within or outside of your industry, of course. These ideas can be pulled into the parsing stages, coming up next.

2. Department opportunities and obstacles are presented in writing to all department heads and the executive team. The usual simplifying, bulking up, and adapting come from individual

review and then group discussion. The product is the list of O&O, which enlivens the grid review that starts next year's Type 5 meeting.

Here's a typical planning calendar for the Type 5 meeting:

◊ June: Directions about content and meeting schedule sent to all department heads and executive team.

◊ July–August: First cut at department O&O; budget planning schedule is due.

◊ September: Packet of department O&O, budget timeline, Type 5 meeting schedule to all.

◊ End of September to Halloween: Company grid, tactical quarterly plan, and draft budget due. (Grid includes the dramatic initiatives from department O&O.)

◊ Halloween to Thanksgiving: Department draft tactical quarterly plans due.

◊ Thanksgiving to December 15: Review and finalize company grid and quarterly plan; quarterly budget due. Departments revise tactical plans.

◊ December 15 to December 20: All finalized.

What about reviews? Use the format of Type 2 and Type 3 meetings to accomplish effective reviews monthly and quarterly. A well-run business reviews financials to budget every month. It reviews progress on programs (customer offerings), initiatives (improvement in narrow areas of focus), and execution of daily business monthly and quarterly. The frequency depends on urgency and the rhythm of improvement; major investment plans may take six months to flesh out, but quarterly or even monthly progress updates will keep obstacles and progress clear.

How You Know When You Need to Redesign

Swimmer Carolyn Wood won an Olympic gold medal in the 1960 Olympics. At fourteen, she was best in the world. Before she was twelve, she visualized herself on the Olympic medal podium. A willing athlete, she loved the hardware (medals, trophies) that came with winning age-group swimming races. After piling up medals and trophies as a fifty-meter sprinter and butterfly swimmer (early star using the new "dolphin kick"), she got a new coach who aimed her for the US Olympic tryouts. Remember: At this stage she's twelve or thirteen years old, living at home. The new coach demanded three shocking changes:

◊ Compete in the butterfly, not her favorite.

◊ Be a backup in the 100-meter freestyle (even though she was ranked number two in the nation).

◊ Change her start, diving over a pole held over the water so high she could clear it only after weeks of agonizing practice.

Yes, she mastered the new start, and yes, she credits it with ramping up her speed yet again. But when the coach required the changes, she was already at the top in US swimming.[3]

The ironic truth is that successful growth requires routinizing most processes to ensure consistent performance with varying people in changing jobs. That hum of consistency, so comforting as it replaces the herky-jerky early stages of growing companies, is the anesthetic numbing both vision and confidence to risk big new success. Entropy is wired in.

The better your systems and culture are, the more likely entropy will cripple your company. Success is the arthritis of good companies. Excelling feels so good that it sets up the creeping slippage that can erupt into shocking disaster. It's not the known problems; the best cultures have systems to catch them. It's the surprise problems, the equivalent of metal fatigue in airplane wings—invisible, then dismissed as a one-off, then denigrated as too small to chase—diluting strength and effectiveness.

> *Failure is not fatal, but failure to change might be.*[4]
>
> —*Legendary USC coach John Wooden*

Harvard's Clayton Christensen popularized the problem in a landmark study of tech behemoth Intel. Its thesis is that as a company grows, "the next big thing" must be unrealistically big to gain attention, let alone investment. If your annual revenue is $59 billion, a new business that promises $400 million is a gnat, less than 1 percent of the parent's sales. Most great opportunities slip by, unnoticed. The focus instead is to buy a large firm in the hope that "synergies" will accelerate growth and inoculate against failure. The data is that 60 to 80 percent of mergers don't increase company value. The news is that this blindness happens often in successful companies much smaller than Intel.

Whether you're facing a dangerous challenge or just the usual entropy, what's the smart way forward? The antidote is to build in a constant search for the next quantum opportunity. If the opportunity comes wrapped in an exploding problem, how do successful leaders approach it?

One of my clients is a successful real estate developer who also builds his own buildings. Growth and a flood of new opportunity began submerging the quality of his company's work—a key competitive advantage. Next, he:

◊ Went to several job sites to see the problems for himself.

◊ Asked each key leader what his group would need to handle 50 percent more business.

◊ Reviewed those requests in his full leadership group.

◊ Found new ways to:

　» Share parts of the work and organize the follow-through.

  » Change parts of the leadership structure to fill unmet needs.

  » Split some jobs and create others.

◊ Planned to build a division that could fill unmet needs in the current organization.

◊ Identified key training needs.

◊ Identified changes in major processes: job descriptions, financial planning and analysis, project management.

Here's a simple frame that will usually work well to get you started. Occasionally, these steps won't be enough, and success will require other actions. But first:

1. Is it true? Problems hit leaders daily, like spaceships hit by meteorites. Usually, they are exaggerated. Taking the hits means coping without much investment, following these steps, which ask, "How do you know?"

2. Ignore it until you hear it from several sources.

3. Check the data. Train your leaders to bring data when they raise a problem.

4. Go to the source if you can. Nothing beats seeing for yourself.

5. How often has it happened?

6. How will it impact us?

7. What do we do now? Be slow to change strategy but quickly adjust tactics.

If tsunami-size problems aren't washing into your reception area, here's your other tactic: The moral isn't that when you're on top, you need to rip it up and start over (Andy Grove's paranoia notwithstanding). Instead, winners develop a constant laser site for quantum opportunity, especially when it requires disciplined adjustment over time. The magic word is "quantum." Most organizations are lousy at that because the busyness and allure of current success subverts their will to jump higher to reward marginal improvement (and properly so).

Instead, create a hard-wired look for breathtaking opportunity. Build into your three-to-five-year strategic plan the expectation that the search for breathtaking opportunity is constant, formal, and articulated in every annual plan. As entrepreneur Larry Pexton said, "When you spot a great opportunity on your plate, stab it before it gets away."[5]

Because the search can't be delegated to a "planning team" unless you have Intel-size resources, here are the steps for ordinary mortals:

Sell the concept to your top leaders. They already have full-time jobs balancing incremental improvement with daily operations; their bonuses, reviews, and daily conversations reinforce that focus. After all, you've built that focus into your successful company. Show examples from other companies, describe in alive terms the benefits, and open the door to compensation and recognition as dramatic as the new opportunity.

Resist the pull of an acquisition. That's a cop-out, usually producing moderate returns at great personal and financial cost.

Specifically include the quantum button in every annual plan. Like every other item, it needs to be described, planned, reviewed, celebrated, and so forth.

Emulate 3M, whose innovation is ranked just behind Apple and Google.[6] **3M built innovation into its culture in many dimensions, including annual celebrations of innovation, a separate Innovation Center in the company, and paid work time set aside for creative thinking.** Emulate this continuing commitment in time, treasure, and recognition, instead of hoping to run into the quantum button on your way to a meeting. It won't be found unless there's a real search built into your mission.

Emulate Intuit. The thirty-four-year-old accounting/ tech business is now a $5 billion company with revenue up 24 percent in 2016 versus 2011, and financial performance in the ninety-ninth percentile of all public companies. Their secret is a focus like 3M, but with special tools:

◊ Dig into findings that "make no sense." Instead of avoiding them, actively search out what they are and how pervasive they are. Example: A special version of Intuit used by gig economy (shared cars, homes, etc.) entrepreneurs.

◊ The "Follow me home" initiative sends a pair of employees to observe customers using their products, currently at about 10,000 hours per year.

◊ "Tiny teams" are groups of three people with intensive training by the CEO, tasked with developing a new process or service.[7] When digging into findings that make no sense uncovered the unserved gig economy entrepreneurs, a tiny team worked out how to serve the new customers.

Search relentlessly. Convert the search from "once in a blue moon" to "something we do here." Bring it alive in quarterly reviews by asking, "What should we do about this that would make a big difference?" when you talk with folks about their current work situation. If you don't ask, you won't receive.

Chapter 5

The Right Things at the Right Time

The costliest mistake that leaders make is failure to delegate. It drowns leaders in the daily trivia sprouting from "failure to ship," which means loss of cash and risk of business failure, especially for businesses with sales up to $500 million (SMEs). Remarkably, the simple decision to delegate fuels powerful growth in leaders and their businesses, even as it multiplies uncertainty and stress.

Verne Smith led an organization of a thousand-plus meat-cutters in 150 Chicago-area Jewel Food Stores, when meat was still cut in the stores. As a very young trainee, I watched Verne in his office plan his day:

◊ Dump the bottom desk drawer in the wastebasket.

◊ Dump the middle drawer into the bottom drawer.

◊ Dump the top drawer into the middle drawer.

◊   Dump his inbox (full of memos) into the top drawer.

◊   Me to Verne with horror: "What are you doing!?"

◊   Verne to me with a grin: "They can phone me if they want me."

The point, for those still marveling at a world with memos: Verne had built leaders who would do the right thing, surrounded with a system that framed their responsibilities, detailed correct practices, and measured their performance. He delegated daily operations to them, and then checked and coached as needed to maintain performance momentum. He knew better than anyone what his teams needed to thrive.

When should a CEO or top leader delegate? The idea is to build a system that thrives on delegation and dictate as little as possible.

What's your balance of dictating versus delegation? Next week track each transaction with D (Delegated) or d (dictated) for three days (usually your busiest). Tally the totals each week, and figure the percentage delegated. Repeat for two more weeks. Combine the results. Your goal is 75 percent D and 25 percent d.

WHEN TO DELEGATE AND WHEN TO DICTATE

Regardless of the result, work on sharper goals or more skilled leaders, and immediately delegate more. What happens when you delegate more? You quickly see where reinforcements are needed. The results often stop the debate, which enables the strengthening you want.

Leadership Tip: Ask your key leaders to do this measure for four weeks and schedule a sharing of scores and their actions to improve.

The Secret Measure

Delegation is the best quick measure of organizational strength that I've seen. If you compare operating statements, customer ratings, and growth, the higher the D, the more likely the organization will be eating its competition's lunch. Why? It launches more employees toward key goals than any other formula; ownership fuels pride that drives to the goal line. It moves the leader to coaching, multiplying his skill and knowledge through many people, instead of keeping him in the game as the main player, limited by his capacity. And it lasts because it forces development of other leaders, and because it doesn't depend on the leader's energy to row the company boat.

When to dictate (other than a fire):

◊ When there isn't time for your team to repair its mistake.

◊ When there is a huge unexpected risk, outside the norm.

What to dictate. It's divided between specifying and approving. "Specifying" means scheduling the work and defining the outcome. "Approving" launches subordinates who have agreed on targets and plans with the CEO to move to accomplish the plans. Hurdles or deviation pull the CEO back in as helper to the owner of the activity. The more the balance is toward approving/advising and away from specifying, the stronger the team, and usually the better the results.

From Dictate to Delegate

The trap is sliding from "what" to "how" in the mistaken belief that the leader knows the best way to implement the priority. Not only is this seldom the case, but a regular diet of "here's how to do it" from the boss will drive your best people out the door in stunning numbers.

.Future leaders grow up being praised for what they do individually, but often flounder as they shift toward leading. Peter Drucker is still right: The leader's job is to get the right things done. It seldom is to do them. The trick is to find the balance. Sort your inbox into three piles:

1. Delete: forget it.
2. Delay: put it aside; your people will fix it if needed.
3. Delegate: needs to be done. Yes, delegate everything.

Now fear jumps into your lap, whispering that only *you* can fix it. Instead, ask these power questions:

1. What do you think we should do?
2. What will it take?
3. How will we measure progress?
4. When will we be done?

Once begun, delegating means helping as little as possible but checking regularly on progress to look for problems, and providing help only as needed to get past the problems.

Check in according to the skill of the person who has the project. More skill = less checking, and the converse is also true.

Dictation leadership does damage in the following ways:

◊ It drowns initiative in others. Why step out? Just wait to be told; it's safer.

◊ It confuses most leaders because it collides with their plan (that you approved).

◊ It erodes communication lines; unless it's direct from the boss, it doesn't matter.

◊ It creates a wasteland after your order is carried out. What now?

◊ It adds to your workload because you now own problems with the follow-up.

Still fighting it? Here's the real rule: *Whenever you dictate, you've failed.*

Corollary: *The growth of your company (in profit) is inversely related to how little work you do yourself.* Yes, the less you do, the more successful your company will be.

Delegation is the most misunderstood critical skill in the leader's toolbox. It's not a handoff; it's a way to powerfully and quickly multiply your team. The foundation is their conviction that you will always delegate to them—*always*. Of course, excellence is expected every time.

Once you've handed over the responsibility, you can become a helper. Until you do, you're a dangerous dictator.

Every leader has three jobs:

1. Grow leaders who deliver results.

2. Set priorities.

3. Manage risk.

The foundation of delegation is active accountability, which means that you and your team know that you'll check on progress, expect problems, and count on them to drive to success with whatever help is needed. You *never* take the ball. Like a great coach, you prepare and guide your team to win. Let's look at the formula.

First comes the setup:

1. Pick the team.

2. Surgically define the outcome and the fences.

3. Get agreement on the timeline.

4. Schedule checkpoints.

Adjust and finish:

1. Check as planned, asking, "How are we doing?" and "What do we need?"

2. Knock down doors to get your team what they need (and no more).

3. Steps 1–4 can be done in less than a half hour. If it isn't done, your odds stink.

MEASURING THE ROI OF PEOPLE DEVELOPMENT

This is about knowing when to hold 'em and when to fold 'em. Only the wisest leaders invest in their people instead of talking about it. The rest do what one client did: "Well I needed to keep him from looking for a job with another company, so we sent him to some training!" Fortunately, months later an outside coach helped this former team leader prepare for a spectacular five-year career marked by success in leading three different departments: engineering, production, and sales. Of course, he's talented and worked hard.

Don't you have at least two or three folks like that in your organization? If not, get them this year, and find them a job. As Bear Bryant, legendary Alabama football coach said, "Get the winners into the game."[1] How does a company get the winners into the game?

Take this culture test to see if you're even trying. Rate each statement true or false as they apply to your top leaders. Total your *T*s and *F*s, and check your score at the end. Answer how it is, not how you'd like it to be.

1. They'll pick up what they need just by working here.

2. Things are fine; don't rock the boat.

3. We need them in their current jobs right now.

4. We can't afford to train for jobs until we need to fill them.

5. I learned it the hard way, and it's working for me.

6. We don't have time or money to do skills assessments.

7. We can teach machine or accounting processes, but we can't teach leadership.

8. People who want to learn will find a way.

9. People are either leaders and managers or they aren't.

10. We're doing okay. How much better will it really be?

11. We can measure the return on a machine, but a person? Not so much.

12. We've got every position filled with a capable person.

How did you score? If there are more than three *T*s, you're grinding to a halt, vulnerable to competitors.

Look at your favorite NBA team. There are three truths in the NBA:

1. Gifted coaches consistently seem to do better (San Antonio Spurs).

2. Teams with average players finish in the bottom half.

3. Top teams constantly bring in players and send them out.

You don't have to be the best leader in the world to be successful, but if you have a mediocre team or worse, you're doomed. Excellent teams have excellent players playing in the best positions for them and the team. It's simple. Apply that to your business.

Find Your Players

The excellent players are only in two places: within your business or outside it. Why not look both places?

In your business, do this simple procedure annually, without fail. Rate each leader with a single letter that combines job performance and work discipline:

A = Exceptional

B = Good, reliable

C = Needs improvement

Evaluate your scores. If all are rated the same, repeat the exercise with clearer instructions. Spot outstanding leadership potential by checking for these strengths, which come from studies of genius:

◊   Works well with others.

◊   Unusually perceptive.

◊   Works hard.

◊   Makes connections rapidly across unrelated information.

◊   Consistently delivers good results on time.[2]

Unless all five are present, odds of success as a senior leader are slim.

If you're looking for players outside your business, make it your business to meet and know the best players at your competition. They may be young, unproven, and driven, not yet a superstar. Think broadly. Look beyond your direct competition to companies known for superb talent. Their weakness often is the problem of hanging on to talent when there's top talent blocking their upward movement.

Grow Your Players

Respond to their scores (as demonstrated in the following paragraphs), in addition to the next individual development step or training:

A players. There should be at least one in every department. If not, get one or grow one. Craft a three-year plan with each of them that's focused on their goals and the help to get there. Spend more of your leadership time and thought on these people because they are setting the pace for the company.

B players. If this is an A-potential person, find out what it will take to get them there; it's either training or reassignment. The person may be in a job that demands skill in a weak area or is new. The personality-conflict explanation is seldom the real reason, although occasionally it's a contributor. Sometimes a B player will be a *B* player. If they are contributing well, appreciate them and keep them challenged. They don't need to become an A player.

C players. Choose the path you'll take with them. Some C players will always be plodders, so put them in plodder jobs because some plodders are fundamental to business success. If they might have potential, identify specific growth areas with those people, track it monthly, and give them half the time to become a B that you think it should take. If their C rating is a cover for unsatisfactory performance, see "Pull Weeds" on page 111.

Move Them

Put A or B players into new roles where they shine. When they've mastered the current role at 75 percent, start looking for their next place to contribute. Yes, create positions for them, usually by collecting portions of existing jobs to match their next development need. The strongest companies put their strongest people in jobs with the highest impact on company results. They do this even when their strongest people demonstrate a technical knowledge gap. They've learned before, and they'll learn again. Don't wait.

Pull Weeds

When people fall short, follow these three steps, always in writing:

◊ Tell them what they need to step up to acceptable performance, with a target date.

◊ At the target date, determine if they have improved enough or they haven't. If yes, praise and ask them to build on their improvement. If no, give them thirty days to meet the targets.

◊ At thirty days, they either stay in their jobs because they've improved enough, or they move to another position, within or outside of the company. Move them to positions that they can likely do well, if possible. If not, thank them for their service and see them out of the business.

Act

Without exception, every leader I've talked with has admitted to moving too slowly much more than moving too fast. The difference is that if you move, there's probably room to adjust. If you hover over the nest, nothing hatches. You can get advice from your best advisors before you move, but move when you're 75 percent sure, not 105 percent.

THE PROS AND SIGNIFICANT CONS OF EMPLOYING FAMILY MEMBERS

Jerry started working with his dad in their manufacturing business when he was a kid. He went on to become its successful president, with a helicopter and forty-four-foot boat for him and his wife, Susan, to enjoy. Susan was another matter. For a while she did well, but as the business grew, the stress of managing finances and office staff worried her enormously. When I met Jerry, he confided that he was sleeping less than two hours a night, and he and his wife fought daily at home and at the office, to their mutual chagrin. When he brought in an outside office manager, his wife resisted at first, understandably reluctant to give up control to someone new. Only as she stepped into a new role as his partner in ownership, and they hired a VP of operations, did the business and their marriage stabilize. They took their first vacation in eleven years, and five years later, they sold the business for more than they dared to imagine.

This happy story hides the complex difficulties that accompany family members in a business.

Three explosive issues are usually present in a business that includes more than one family member:

1. Parental fantasy. Early-stage business building is like observing your kids' early adolescence or the early relationship with your spouse. Hope, essential for powering through tough times, obscures reality in the foggy desire that your family member will be an exceptional contributor to the business. The facts usually disappoint. The question is only about the damage to the business and the family.

2. Adding a family member as an employee, regardless of competence or desire, multiplies the risk of family pain, dilutes essential business culture, and adds complexity that risks the success of the business. Picture the juggler who moves his juggling act to the high wire at Cirque du Soleil.

3. Succession, especially for the CEO and primary owners, has been well discussed in the literature. The hidden problem is for him or her to grasp and implement the necessary shifts in role from leader to advisor. Without that shift, the business will die or be sold, but denial and habit powerfully work against both. The hidden shift is the declining power and influence that successful succession demands. More bluntly, in

early years, employees do what they are told; in later years, the advisor is limited to occasional suggestion. The path is familiar, like parenting: significant power in early years to occasional powerless guidance as the child moves into her twenties. The trick, seldom mastered alone, is knowing where one is along the line and what spot optimizes results for the business. The two are seldom the same. It is much more fraught if the successor CEO is a child, because of the inevitable emotional riptides.

Critical insight: Supplement your basic three advisors (CPA, attorney, financial) with a dream team of outside professionals experienced in the sweep and complexity of business strategy and operations. Otherwise, your key advisors join you in not knowing what you don't know. The basic three advisors' deep skills are essential to your success, but their peripheral vision is often impaired by success in their narrow field and limited exposure to the complexity that you face as CEO. Ask these outside professionals regularly for tough insights to penetrate the fog of business as usual so that you can see clearly what is needed next.

After all that, if you still insist on adding family members to your business, then consider the three stages of the process with all their implications.

Stage 1: Bringing Family into the Business

Employing your son, daughter, or other relative in your business may be the worst investment you'll ever make. It's high risk financially and emotionally, the odds of pain are high, and the business results often will fall short of the contribution that a skilled nonfamily member delivers. Yes, folks do it all the time, and yes, it appears to work. But as a wag said, "You're comparing their outside with your inside." The other owner's experience looks okay from the outside, and problems too often are dismissed as unique family dynamics. Hiring your relative is much like addiction. It's unfamiliar at first, then it's wonderful, and then it's impossible to get away—or nearly. Like a teenager, you think, "It won't happen to us," until it does. Let's cut through it: An owner who hires a relative is doing it mostly for himself or herself, not for the relative.

Disregard these rules for hiring a relative at your peril:

1. Start with the health of your business, not the possible contributions of your family member. Most businesses succeed or fail because of what their people do or don't do, not what their machines do. How can you tell? If there's a problem with a customer, you wouldn't allow it to be blamed it on a machine, would you? If the machines are operating directly with your customers, then you'd look at how they were set up, their weak spots, and so forth. You would expect that a worker would intervene to prevent a problem or solve it. That means that your employees matter. A lot. So your rule for hiring is about what the employee can deliver to the business, not the reverse.

2. Hire any qualified relative before they are age twenty-five in a menial job with a boss that respects you enough to require your relative to perform. Set a termination date when they start, and require a written evaluation from the employee and boss of no more than one page (it should include three sections: strengths, weaknesses, learnings).

3. Tell every relative that they must successfully work at another firm for three to five years and be promoted at least twice. More is better. They must provide a performance evaluation from that employer before you'll consider them.

4. Explain that you can only hire them if there's a real job opening in the company.

5. Use an ownership meeting (meeting of owners) to evaluate the relative versus the other best candidate for the job, and may the best person be hired. If possible, turn down your relative's job application at least twice, and be specific about the skills they need to develop to be considered.

6. Use an ownership meeting to clarify your purpose in hiring the relative. If it's mostly about family, be clear about that in the meeting.

7. To avoid crippling your relative, assign him or her to your toughest manager, with the express requirement that they earn his or her respect. That respect is a requirement for further employment or promotion.

If by now you're nodding your head and saying, "We're doing all that," then ask someone you trust (your dream team?) to audit what's really happening with the family employee. Are all seven rules being followed? Are *you* willing to follow them?

Stage 2: Running the Business and the Spirit Problem

The spirit problem exists as soon as the second employee is hired, relative or not. The spirit problem is that as the leader, regardless of title, your opinions guide any employee who's been with the company a month or more. In fact, you exist in their heads as a fully formed person with specific opinions about everything in the business.

The first transaction: The employee looks at a task and asks himself, "What would the boss want?" The question is a problem, but the bigger problem is the employee's imagination, which decides what the boss would want and enacts it. Never mind that the employee has no idea what the boss really wants.

The second transaction: The employee starts training an employee and asks, "What would the boss want?" As before, the trainer applies a mix of personal experience, her own training, and her imagination about the boss to spell out how a job is to be done. Until the boss checks, he doesn't know what the employee thinks he thinks!

The third transaction: The employee, now a senior executive, makes a difficult and complex decision, secure in the knowledge that the boss would do it the way he just did it. When the boss discovers the decision and disagrees profoundly, the mess from the "boss ambush" can stretch from fear by the employee to a rush of powerlessness that sticks like gum to a shoe. The "boss ambush" is well meaning and inevitable because leaders' views on complex issues will vary.

Stage 3: Turning Over Leadership to a Family Member

The spirit problem is a modest challenge until the leader wants to step back. Stepping back requires either a new leader or selling the business.

Hiring a relative to become president or CEO means moving him through all departments in the business and requiring success in each. With proper preparation and an authentic willingness to continue to learn, the new CEO may have a chance to succeed. The problem is that because his mom or dad ran the business, his decisions will be influenced by his memory of what the parent "would" do. That memory may drive either compliance or rebellion, but the problem is the same: the outsize influence of the parent. It's good in theory—the parent has wisdom—but unless this memory is updated with the current reality, it's almost always a liability.

A manufacturing company was successful for twenty-five-plus years, through ups and downs, but finally dissolved into bankruptcy because the son couldn't see past his dad's practice of cutting employees to the level that current sales would support. The problem was that he didn't move past the cutting to pump new life into the business, either by borrowing money for operating capital or investing in sales growth. He didn't seem to see what he didn't see. Excruciating.

But then consider this killer question: What is the new role of the current CEO, and what is the path for him and the relative to reach their respective positions (likely, the current CEO becomes chairman)? This vital dance too often focuses on the replacement person and not nearly enough on the tough task of the incumbent to reinvent himself and his role in the company that he's devoted his life to building. This dance juggles the continued health of the business and its employees, funding retirement for the exiting CEO, and threading the path of a parent and leader with a son or daughter.

There is little expert guidance, other than legal and financial, provided for the retiring CEO by his long-term advisors. Neither is sufficient. It's not about the technical land mines, although they need attention. It is about a man or woman who has succeeded for years by being in charge, assessing risk and acting, being in the pilot's seat. Riding in the back of the plane is so unfamiliar that it breeds unhealthy reactions.

What's a former pilot to do? Get expert help in the form of a mentor who will tell the truth. Then follow these steps:

◊ Write a letter to the new CEO outlining your confidence in and expectations of them. Hand it to them and take yourself out the door.

◊ Ask the new CEO how you can be helpful, both in form and content.

◊ Suggest this framework, because neither of you is experienced at this.

◊ Types of situations where you might be helpful in the "how," but not the "whether":

» Major investment.

» Major hiring.

» Firing high-level senior person.

» Major restructuring.

Yes, you're available when the stakes are high if you'll limit your advice to asking or suggesting questions to aid in the decision. As soon as you shift to prescribing from questioning, the historic fog of your relationship will dilute your wisdom and put the decision at risk.

How can you construct situations where you can be together without the business being the topic on the table? For some, this is a nonstarter. For others, it's a powerful placebo to deal with the very real loss of your position, power, and respect. Your greatest risk may be that you are unwilling to live the life you now have and try to sneak back to power. Some do, but often at eye-watering cost to family and the business.

Chapter 6

The Power of Relationships

Relationships are the fulcrum of action in successful organizations. They provide connections, communication links, feedback loops, and high-speed data analytics to fuel the performance of your people.

ACHIEVING ENGAGEMENT

Much is written about relationships, yet many relationships wrestle with unnecessary friction. Necessary disclaimer: Yes, no good relationship is always smooth. It's not about whether there is friction, but whether the expectation is that the friction will be resolved. Unresolved friction blocks the power of relationships out of fear, but the expectation of resolution enables attempts to resolve both the problem and the friction. The guidance is to seek rapid resolution while maintaining the debate. The challenge is that trust enables action, even resolution, pulled along by mutual drive to reach shared goals. Where trust is tenuous, what's an alternative?

Negative Engagement

Leaders as far back in history as the Roman Empire relied upon a threatening "outside enemy" to rally their people to a common cause. The relationship was more about the enemy than the team, but it worked. Even today, leaders can rally their people despite disagreement if they can frame "outside" (company) goals that everyone can support. This action narrows activity to paths to reach the outside goals despite personal friction. This could be labeled "negative engagement" because it's not about resolving personal differences but about mutual goals.

A classic example of this is in the departmental friction between sales and production, or production and engineering. Each pairing has built-in friction points by job definition. Sales will push for orders and be pulled to make promises that are tough to fulfill, such as shipping dates, order quantities, or even certain product specifications. Production will try to stretch shipping dates, reducing inventory or managing production schedules to meet their own objectives. Engineering will focus on product performance to the detriment of "manufacturability" or will reject a potential supplier because of inadequate quality-control systems when that supplier's product is essential to meet a production goal.

This friction is the natural result of the departments' drive to meet their goals, producing friction inevitably in the usual course of business. It's not about evil motives or even greed. It comes from a combination of strong drive to succeed and little emphasis upon shared solutions. It's not that they don't talk about it; it's that their leaders aren't required to be accountable to company goals. Instead, departments are measured, recognized, and sometimes paid on their individual performance, with little incentive or informal pressure to resolve friction damaging to the company.

If your people are doing this, there are three actions open to you:

1. Ignore it, hoping that the noise will subside. Your results likely will follow the noise.

2. Ask the leaders of colliding departments to get together and work it out. In many cases, stating the problem clearly with both in the room and telling them that it's their job to resolve it will be enough. Make it clear that you're available to help if they wish.

3. Initiate a work session with the two and lead the discussion. A client CEO described a meeting where closet finger-pointers are put in a room with their boss, asked to frame their concerns, and then asked to resolve them to the good of the company. It usually works, but the key is the executive who calls both to the room, owns the responsibility to frame the discussion, holds it as

tension rises, and asks each to find an alternate path that returns to progress instead of fighting. Here is how to do this procedure yourself, step by step:

» Decide to defuse. Demonstrate clear benefits to the discussion before it is set up. If the benefits are small, skip it. Not all problems should be solved.

» Interview individually. Even if you think you understand the people and the disagreement, do this step because if you skip it, the odds of continuing friction go through the roof.

» Ask targeted questions of each person, and take notes. Pull back from your frustration and harness your empathy. You need to have it and exhibit it to help make this approach work.

Sample Script

It seems that you and Joe are struggling with timely reporting of problems. Is that what you see?

Could you describe the problem, so I can picture it as you do?

Why is this a problem for you?

Is it worth it to resolve it? If not, why not?

What will you lose if this isn't resolved?

What is in the way of finding a solution with him?

If he were sitting here, what would you ask him to do?

If he does that, what are you willing to do to resolve things?

Would you be willing to talk about it with him and me together?

Sit together, the three of you, and follow a script like this:

Thank you for getting together. Each of you says he wants to resolve this. Would each of you describe the problem, one at a time? John, would you go first? Bill, you and I will listen closely and take notes.

Why does this matter to you, personally?

[Repeat with Bill.]

One at a time: *Now, what are you willing to do to resolve it? What do you want him to do on his end?*

Are you willing to give it a try?

What will you do when the problem comes back? (Ask each of them.)

If you get stuck again, may I join you to help?

Let a pause live while you count to twenty-five. It might take a minute or two for the conversation to continue. If there's a flare of feeling, acknowledge it: *Bill, this is tough for you to sit through.* If one won't offer a solution after three minutes of silence, say: *You know, it sounds like there's more here than meets the eye.* Pause for up to three minutes.

Your state of mind and behavior matters in this. Being their boss may be of little value in unlocking the jam. Instead, try deference.[1] Deference means that you show respect to a person and even submit to their preference where possible, as though they are your superior, even though they are not. It doesn't equate to weakness. It shows the highest possible respect for their position, and strangely, when you do that, you are more likely to be pulled into a valid discussion of what their position really looks like from inside their head. Instead of reciting to yourself all their annoying habits, lean back upon deference to allow them to bring their ideas into the room. Once there, the ideas can be discussed and supported, changed, or moved to the side. Until they are in the room, they exist beyond your reach at full temperature.

This approach is powerful, if you're willing to own your own power, which is substantial. Your power is in your willingness to invite the conversation and let it flow with minimum guidance. It is likely that when the real reasons appear, you'll find that the path to resolution will emerge from questions like these: *What would that look like? How would we start that? What do you want to do first?* Now you're on the way to a lower temperature and smoother solution.

Providing Empowerment

Forgive me, but I don't know a better word. "Empowerment" needs to be sent away, along with useless appendages such as "curated" and "artisanal," as examples of words flogged until empty. Let's rebirth "empowerment" as other people's ownership of their personal power. Imagine the surge in performance if most folks used most of their gifts most of the time!

How many of us know someone (besides ourselves) who seems to hold themselves back, either through shyness, guilt, or a misunderstanding of humility. It is naïve to think that someone will discover your secret good works or to dissemble when praised, "Oh, it was nothing." Here are four steps to help people begin to own their power.

Empowerment Step 1

When you spot a good job, say so out loud or in a brief note. If the person who did the work dissembles, immediately respond to right the ship. Say, "It *was* something, and it helped a lot. Thank you!" Move on, and don't chew over it anymore. Instead, teach him (and onlookers) that it's good to do a good job and okay to accept praise with your head up. Sometimes it helps to put it into words: "When someone says that you did a good job, say thank you!"

Empowerment Step 2

When you find what looks like a problem, ask, "What happened?" Look for facts. Never mind who did it. Instead ask how it happened and what can be done to prevent it next time. Stop there. If you keep the focus on a problem that can be repaired, you'll avoid criticizing the person, which seldom yields improvement. Even when the person made a mistake, say something like,

"Well, that didn't work very well, did it? What should we do next time?" We all know that we make mistakes, but if we're personally degraded when the inevitable happens, we burrow back into our self-doubt and step away from the risk of trying something unfamiliar. One of the common company myths is that everyone knows more than I do. In fact, most people are learning some portion of their job, which means that they haven't mastered it yet. If your stance is that we're all learning, then your questions will be about learning and doing better, instead of about who did the dumb thing.

Empowerment Step 3

Avoid taking credit unless it clearly and entirely was up to you. If you helped, give credit to the other person first. Be known as a person who looks for solutions instead of one who looks for recognition (or worse, avoids blame). See that credit goes to the person or team that deserves it whenever possible. Shift your picture of yourself from powerful leader to a person around whom things happen. The connection isn't always clear, but it seems that your teams and initiatives do well much of the time.

Empowerment Step 4

When there is a cross-department problem, be a coalition builder instead of a provocateur. Go to individuals who will be key to find a solution and implement it (sometimes these are different folks), and ask if you can work with them on the project. Asking permission is a way of showing respect. Once you've collected the team in this way, you can suggest a work session and begin to ask questions to move the project forward. In general, "askers" get support more quickly than "tellers" because they must attend to the other opinions in the room. This approach also frequently is a faster path to a better solution.

EMPOWERMENT IN ACTION

In a manufacturing company where I worked, the CFO was also in charge of operations. He was a stellar person, but his dairy farm background led him to measure people by how many hours they worked—and he was skeptical of most people's intentions. He tried to use "routings" (job timings) to schedule work and measure productivity. He knew that his production people changed the reported times to be easier on themselves, so he changed them back to make the standards produce good earnings. Translation: If you add up the standard times to produce a product, they should equal the actual hours to produce it. They never did, and his projections were wrong; he and the crew didn't trust each other, and results were lousy until a new production manager measured actual hours and stopped using the distorted routings. The connection: He "asked" how long it should take, measured it, and asked what would make things work better. His assumption was that his team wanted to do better. They did.

Empowerment may be best described as the bicycle and driving technique. In both cases, a young person learns when they get on the bicycle or behind the wheel, not by listening in class (although that helps). What works is letting them try, gently correcting only when necessary, and letting them see the result of what they did.

As a leader, I can't "give" people power or force them to use their gifts. That is a bit like making a rose grow. I can plant in the right soil with the right amount of sunlight, water, and fertilizer; I can prune and spray. I can invite, encourage, and, especially, create a good environment for that plant, but I don't make it grow. People are at least as individual as plants.

Empowerment is individual, even among teams. An unspoken error is expecting that team-building will enhance the empowerment and performance of everyone on the team. It won't. Empowerment is like a booster shot for team-building. It won't hurt those fully engaged, but it will lift the saggers and give them the energy and even excitement to be powerful contributors too!

Likewise, many commonly prescribed leadership behaviors will lift the minimum performance of most people, but today's volatile, uncertain, complex, ambiguous (VUCA) world[2] that jumbles only adequate organizations, demands more in unexpected ways. Minimum acceptable isn't acceptable anymore, and the bar continues to rise.

Empowerment Inventory

Empowerment requires empathetic understanding of what each person needs to thrive. We've already reviewed empathy, of course. The question here is: What is the shortest list of things that *this* person needs to thrive? Once determined, this individual list can then provide clues to what many others need. Just as there are types of fertilizer that work on large groups of roses, certain behaviors will click with many people, even though each person is different from all others.

Here's the process:

1. Discover specific behaviors or situations (influencers) that encourage a person to thrive.

2. Look at and talk with the person to find out what helped provide the lift in their outlook.

3. Ask what else would help them.

4. Observe their work group and others to spot folks who aren't thriving.

5. Ask one of those folks how they are doing, and what would help them.

6. Listen and watch closely.

7. When they light up, write down what they said.

8. Use the thing that lights them up (igniter) explicitly in informal feedback sessions to help them see their strength and look for places to use it.

This process can help spot training needs or folks who need to move to a different position and decode what's behind their slumping performance.

When Oregon Symphony president Scott Showalter joined the organization, its attendance, morale, and financials were sliding, like most symphonies across the country. Three years later, ticket sales are up 55 percent, budget has increased 35 percent, and the number of classical concerts has risen 20 percent. Community engagement expanded dramatically with 20 percent of audiences attending their first concert.[3] What made the difference? Empowerment.

Scott discovered a brilliant show creator stuck inside the limits of his tiny budget. Scott to this person: "Let me worry about the money. You get us programs that will fill the house." They started groundbreaking successes, like screening Harry Potter movies with live sound played by the orchestra, a Stravinsky piece animated by dramatic "puppets" made by the man responsible for *The Lion King* Broadway show's puppets (now in its twentieth year), and more.[4]

MAKING THE TOUGH CALLS

The tough calls are never about financials. They are always about people or your personal pride. The personal pride part can be handled in a frank discussion with your best advisor. (If you don't have one, stop now and get one. No great leader works alone. All seek wise outside observers who care enough to think deeply, and who know enough to contribute effectively.) After talking with your advisor, immediately sit down with your boss or lead investor, and tell him or her where you are with the problem and what you're thinking of doing. Do not wait for a perfect answer. The delay usually costs more in money, personal misery, and organizational mess. As someone said, "Put the dead mouse on the table."

The people part is usually easier outside of yourself than that part inside of yourself. Use this approach:

◊ Confront your guilt about a problem that you apparently can't solve. It's almost always there, so look at it and dump it.

◊ Check to see if it was there before you. If so, you clearly didn't start it. Maybe you can fix it, and maybe not.

◊ Use your advisor to rough out an approach to the outside problem. It will calm the little person inside you that's screaming some form of "You just can't do this job after all!"

◊ Allow a rough plan to help you shift to the outside problem. You can always come back and work on your pride, but it usually retreats in small steps, not at full gallop (although we sometimes wish for the gallop).

Outside of yourself: Look first at the business situation. Use this business power question: What does the business need? Make it part of your toolkit. It isn't permission to cut corners in any way, but rather to clarify what matters to the business, or not. Sometimes the people problem is just annoying to you but working fine in the business. That's not uncommon and can tell you something about yourself. If you discover that it's mostly annoying, check to see if it's getting in the way of what the business needs by distracting others. If so, address it directly and kindly. If not, move on.

Look beyond the person in question to the system that they function in. The problem may be large and involve other leaders in the company, customers, or technical problems. Take your pick. If necessary, sit down with the person and ask, "What's the problem? What's the problem behind it?" Problems that matter are almost always broader than just one person, and that broader problem may be your next stop.

If the person's job is to find a way to fix the situational problems, and they haven't done that, go to the next stage. Ask if he sees what you see. Let him talk, but describe what *you* see and its impact as clearly as possible. It's about the business results, not about who's mad at whom. Don't let juicy gossip get in the way.

Now, if after all that, it's still clearly the person that's the problem, here's your action roadmap. Do you train the person, or replace them?

Train folks who want to do the job but lack the tools, skills, experience. If you're unsure, ask their supervisor or one of their coworkers who's proven to report what she sees. Give the benefit of the doubt to the employee if you're not sure the training will work. You can't read minds; you may save a good future employee, and all the other employees watch to see what happens to folks who struggle. You want to be a place where folks who struggle are supported and rewarded, instead of a place where struggle produces pain and job loss. That will gut the enthusiasm and willingness to try new things that undergird great companies.

Replace folks after providing:

◊ A clear warning, in writing, that their work is unacceptable.

◊ A period to improve and specific review dates with a supervisor.

◊ Personal training that's worked well for others.

Except for behavior that's considered "termination for cause" (theft, lying, fraud, breaking the law, and so forth), look first for a job inside the company. When it's for cause, get your HR professional to frame a termination process, and do what they say. It will save you time and money.

Replacement means moving that person to a different job. Sometimes it's within the company, sometimes it's outside of it. If the person has failed in two or more assignments within the company, a compelling reason is required to give him another try; otherwise, he needs to move on.

The logic for replacement is that all people have skills and gifts. It is a waste of their one life to have them struggle to do a job they can't do or won't learn. Instead, do what you'd do for a friend: help them out of the dead-end job to one where they can contribute and tell them so.

Finally, when the news you bring will be upsetting, always bring another person with you as a witness (if possible, someone trained in HR). Hand the employee a letter and ask him to read it right then. It will help him through the rush of feelings that can derail the best-planned discussion. The letter should say briefly that his current job is no longer available to him, but that you are offering him a choice of job X within the company or a chance to find another one outside the company. Outline separation terms in another document approved by your HR professional. You may be mumbling that this is all simple and widely known. That may be true, but you'd be amazed at how frequently it's not done (likely in your company as well).

In a company where I worked, one of the machines chopped off pieces of metal to precise dimensions. Yes, "chopped." It had been operated safely for many years and was safe if operated properly. One of our new employees was trained (hands-on by an experienced supervisor) and watched closely until he seemed to be reliably safe. Soon after, he cut off part of his finger. After surgery and healing, he returned to work, had a great deal more training and supervision, and still managed to cut off part of another finger. He was moved to another part of the operation, away from anything that could injure him. Well, after I left the company, things slowed down, and he was part of a large layoff. He next appeared with a lawyer in a deposition, claiming that he hadn't been trained. The company won the lawsuit. The point: This stuff matters a lot. It's vital to closely assess capability and performance, even when it's tough to do.

The path I just described works well in almost any company. It takes more effort than most folks choose because they're swamped with their regular jobs. These processes matter so much because your employees know just about everything that goes on, even the confidential stuff. They do. Instead of trying to hide things, behave as though they know everything. Communicate the reasons behind every tough decision except personnel moves. Personnel moves should be explained as matching people's skills with job needs, period. If there is attitude, personal friction, laziness, or other acting out, people will see it, which negates the need for public explanation.

When there are tough choices because of the financial situation, tell the truth to everyone as soon as you tell the bank. They will appreciate your confidence in them, and they'll surprise you with their ideas and willingness to step up. In the year when I made zero dollars in the real estate business, I admitted to my teenage girls for the first time that I wasn't currently making any money. It was impossibly hard to admit that, but to my surprise their response was, "It's okay, Dad. We'll figure out a way to spend way less money." And they did! Amazing that it took me so long to ask for their help.

When you go dark with the bad news, it grows like a poison weed in the fears of your people. Be known for telling it like it is, promptly.

CHANGING TIMES REQUIRE CHANGING TALENT

Retention isn't what it used to be. That's not because the job market is strong or weak but because accelerating change demands different solutions. Remember VUCA? You're swimming in it but likely barely notice it. Doubt it? When did you get your first computer? How does yours compare today? Facebook is the single largest advertising source in the world in ad dollars. Even if your personal life isn't much different from ten years ago, your world is dramatically different. I dare you to think of something in your life besides vital relationships that hasn't changed in the last ten years.

It matters because your customers live in this changing world and use it as a yardstick to make choices. Your lousy commercials that worked so well in the past are now boring at best, damaging at worst, raising doubts about the competence of your product or service. Your customers measure you against what they see today, not where you've been.

The talent problem is to have folks with the right skills in the right jobs when you need them. A terribly destructive myth is that the best companies seldom "lose" an employee. A walk around reveals folks who "have been with us" for fifteen, eighteen, twenty-one years. Those folks are essential for their unwritten knowledge and commitment to getting the work done. What's new is the requirement that more and more of your team are learners, that they like to learn, will choose an employer because of their chance to learn, and will value that learning near the top of their job preference list. Unless you're a start-up or early stage, most of your employees are maintainers instead of learners. The trick is to change the percentage of maintainers to learners from 80/20 toward 30/70. Yes, I did the numbers right.

Learners are folks who like to learn (mostly) and are willing to risk a new job or project that requires them to learn at firehose speed. You can discover learners by asking questions like:

◊ What are you reading?

◊ What concerts or movies have you seen (other than TV or YouTube)?

◊ What video games are you playing? (Someone on your team can tell you which are the "puzzle" games and which are point-and-shoot. Look for the "puzzles.")

◊ What organizations are you in, and what do you do there?

Ask two of your best learners what they do in their free time. Choose one in their twenties and one in their late forties. Add their activities to your question list. You also look for evidence of persistence and grit (persistence through tough times) to avoid learners who are jumpers: learn and leave.

Here is a grit story from Bruce Cazenave, CEO of Nautilus, when he was a product manager at Black+Decker in the early 1990s:

I had this idea to propose DeWalt [brand for professional tools], the yellow tools and a whole different strategy to launch that. It got shot down fast because one of the guys didn't believe in a separate brand. He wanted the Black+Decker brand to be it. We were pushing water uphill, and it just wasn't going anywhere. He ended up leaving, and the next guy who came in came was from the automobile industry, where you have all these different brands for different purposes. He grabbed it and ran with it. Sure enough, after two years, we were in the marketplace and making hay with it. It was a matter of just learning to be continually pushed and push management. Change helped too.[5]

Note the three things that drove this success:

1. A powerful new brand idea and strategy.

2. The persistence to make the case to top management.

3. A new leader who had a different perspective.

The story of grit and brand are appealing, but the igniter was the new person, not the strength of concept or plan. The point is: When the current team is experiencing a road block, the leader's job is to unblock the talent or bring in a new coach to accomplish it. The talent shift isn't always down in the organization. In fact, if the talent team isn't keeping up with the world, the business must either change the leader's perspective or change the leader to survive.

Surfing looks smooth and graceful. In person it's violent, permanently unstable, and just barely possible even in good conditions. Grace is great, but skill in riding the board decides whether the run ends at the end of the curl or the board drops the rider onto the coral. The ocean is the ocean, and the changing world is the changing world. Your surfers must be able to ride today's surf.

Chapter 7

No One Believes What
They Read or Hear

Leadership is not about communication. It's about meticulous listening at surge speed, linking closely with each person as they talk or write. "I feel you," a rap cliché, is code for "I understand at a deep emotional level." That personal link is a connection that's heart to heart, not just head to head (although that's where it may start). It may be the best description of a super leader.

YOU ARE THE AVATAR

An "avatar" is an exemplar, a symbol that can be a living person. Avatars typically absorb an image that is created by the beliefs of the person who observes it. To make it simple, as a leader you are an example, a living metaphor, and become whatever your employees believe about you. Strangely, their beliefs have more power over their performance than who you really are, unless you let them repeatedly see the real you.

This is bound to collide with your public face, which is a cover for the humanness that you reserve for your kids or your dying sister or your mom. But aren't you the same person at work, at home, and in the hospital? Where is it written that you must change into a different person at work?

So there's proof that you can do this. If you've done it at home or in the hospital or on the field coaching your kids, you can do it again. It's now in the realm of "want to," which you control, pretty much. So much for claiming that this doesn't apply to you.

Research shows that 82 percent of people don't trust the boss to tell the truth.[1] The source, *Edelman's Trust Barometer* for 2013, reports results from 31,000 respondents in twenty-six markets worldwide. After

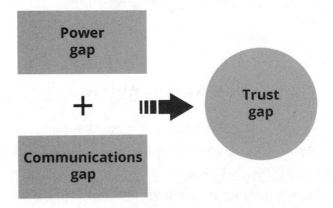

you convince yourself that your own statistics aren't so damaging, just get to the point: There's a trust gap whenever there's a power gap, especially if it's topped with a communication gap. You can do some things to reduce the gap, and reduction is better of course.

We'll insert the mandatory note about discipline to observe that discipline works just fine in a high-connection/high-trust environment. North Carolina and former University of Kansas basketball coach Roy Williams, responsible for years of top-ten teams, routinely has the team to his home for Thanksgiving dinner. Somehow, he's secure in his position as head coach and head disciplinarian. It has worked for years.

In a survey of 1,000 American executives, psychologist Michelle McQuaid found that 65 percent of executives would trade a pay raise for a better boss.[2] But wait, there's more. Fred Rogers hosted *Mister Rogers' Neighborhood,* an iconic children's TV show, for three decades, and won three Emmys and more. If you were a kid or a parent from 1968 to 2000, you likely saw him on TV, softly powerful. Tom Junod in *Esquire* magazine recounted what happened when Fred Rogers accepted his Lifetime Achievement Award in front of the usual crowd gathered for the Emmy Awards: He bowed and said, "All of us have special ones who have loved us into being. Would you just take, along with me, ten seconds to think of the people who have helped you become who you are? . . . I'll watch the time." The crowd swallowed their laughter and then understood that Mister Rogers was serious and expected their cooperation.

As Junod says, "People realized . . . that Mister Rogers was not some convenient eunuch but rather a man, an authority figure who actually expected them to do what he asked."[3]

Remember empathy, one of the five essential leadership skills per the *US Army Field Manual?* You saw it there, and nobody expects you to be Mr. Rogers.

Reducing the Power Gap

So now you're busted. You have it inside you. The question is: Do you have the guts to let it out? But first, let's talk to the voice in your head that says something like, "That's for other people who don't have *my* job or *my* people." Sadly, it's true as long as you want it to be true. If you're still wriggling away, reread what you just read. If you want to get better, here's a starter: Imagine that you could feed magic food to your employees that would light them up, bring them up, enable them to deliver all that's in them. Yes, you can. No, it doesn't work all the time, but it works often enough to make a difference. The doorway to change is reducing the power gap and the communications gap between you the leader and your people.

Here are five steps you can take to reduce the power gap in your organization.

Get over your title. It's an invitation to contribute, not a statement of rank. Colin Powell, one of the highest-ranking generals in the United States, said, "The day soldiers stop bringing you their problems is the day you have stopped leading them. They have either lost confidence that you can help them or concluded that you do not care. Either case is a failure of leadership."[4] If you imagine yourself as helper instead of leader, you're off to a good start.

Don't lean on your ability to fire people. That ability looms in the background of all employees, but it is of tiny consequence to the business. It is not an element of leadership; it's emotional blackmail. If you rely on it, you'll get the response of people who feel blackmailed—all defense and no initiative. Usually, if you must fire a person, it's your failure for hiring them or not training them. Occasionally, folks self-select out, but not often.

Apply railroad leadership. When you walk around, stop, look, and listen (especially listen). You don't have to produce brilliant anything, other than thanks.

When you walk, ask one question at a time, and aim it at just one person. An example might be "What's hard right now?" Listen closely, look closely, decide to be interested, and ask one or two more questions to paint the picture a bit better for you. Your task is to understand something you didn't understand before. It's not to fix anything. If you hear a problem that a supervisor needs to know about, ask if the supervisor has been alerted.

If the answer is no, that's data for you about communication in that team. Store your information for future discussions. It may become part of the fabric of a complex situation that helps find the thread to unravel it.

Apply these techniques in meetings. Especially in meetings, be present to each person as she speaks. That means no phones, no computer, no interruptions from outside the meeting (people, messages, phones, texts—you get the idea). Most vital, bring your brain to the room. Work on other tasks later. People can tell if you're with them. Always. Why would they commit to you when you're only half committed to them?

Note: These aren't groundbreaking ideas unless you're not doing them regularly. *Doing them* is groundbreaking!

Reducing the Communications Gap

We'll reverse it and give you a place to frame your gap-shrinkers. Here are the steps:

1. Picture three of your most vital leaders.

2. Write down one thing you'll do with them. It may be spending fifteen minutes with them, or going for a walk with them, or sitting down with them in their cubes and asking what you can help with (or bringing a topic that you know they are struggling with). Mostly, listen and ask questions.

3. Do it. The point is not to challenge them to produce an answer, it's to introduce them to a new way to use you—as a helper, sounding board, and committed partner. It's *your* task to pull them into the conversation, so go gently into it.

Note: There is nothing here about solving the problem. Nothing. Let the gap shrink. It will.

Content and Process: The Two Aspects of Communication

The test of communication is only "What did the audience hear?" I use "hear" as a broad label for the brain action that processes inputs from all senses into pictures or memories or ideas in the brain. These ideas are what we respond to and what we remember. My memory of a blue rock is different from everyone's memory, even though the rock is the same for everyone.

My dad, who finished his high school education in a tiny Oklahoma town, said that if someone can't read your writing, you might as well not write it. My piano teacher tirelessly reminded us that music was a form of communication. With yourself or others, no communication = no music.

The Content Challenge

The problem with content isn't the audience, it's the writer. Content unlearned is wasted, regardless of the setting. If Einstein hadn't communicated $E=mc^2$, it would be the same as if he had never discovered it. The challenge for most of us is that we work at content, but shoot from the hip regarding communication. The evidence? When you hear a powerful speaker, it's his presentation as much as his content that grabs. And what is it about the presentation? You are pulled into his ideas. Yes, content is vital. The great speaker without content is boring. There, I said it. Now, about your content . . .

The three rules of content:

Rule 1: It's for other people, not you. Test every core idea on someone else. A core idea is the heart of your message. Find people who don't worship you but share your commitment and understanding of the situation. Push past your reluctance to be called out as missing the target. See if they effortlessly get it. Probe to discover which part they missed or found pointless or boring (or however it misses the mark). Ask why. Use their ideas to sharpen your content.

Rule 2: Present the truth, period. This is career threatening. There are "stretchers," and there are "diggers." Stretchers embellish and exaggerate a bit. Diggers present a wearying fabric of evidence that can't be grasped without outrageous work. If you feel very smart after crafting content for a presentation, check it out with someone. Your power is in the simple light you wield, not the complexity of your story. You're not writing a high school essay here. Neither stretcher nor digger is a compelling storyteller because their content is either suspect or impenetrable. Telling the truth simply is a rare gift. It will distinguish your content. Ask yourself, "What is the most powerful truth in my message?" In this instance, "powerful" translates to impact on essential results.

Rule 3: Make it simple. Most powerful ideas are simple. It's when people try to power them up by adding capes and jet belts that the light gets blocked. Start by writing down the takeaway: What single idea do you want your audience to take with them? It doesn't matter whether you've heard this before. If you don't do it every time as a separate step, your communication will be weak. If you have more than three takeaways, you've lost your audience. They'll choose to retain what interested them, which might be a random thought entirely outside the discussion. Watch their eyes: Do they get it?

The Process Challenge

Communicating is a skill and an art. If you think you're so good that you don't need the tools of great presenters, I dread your presentations. Great communicators work at communication as much as content. Every time.

Joth Ricci, a successful serial CEO, talked about "distraction management" when I spoke with him.[5] He's referring to keeping the organization on track toward its goals, instead of wandering after the next appealing thing. Apply this in your presentation. Look for the through line, the logical sequence of ideas and illustrations that stay on point. Examples and pictures each must serve the main message. Intriguing stories that stray are left out. Always. The search for entertainment can misguide even the best of us. The best of us don't succumb. Tell the entertaining story some other time.

Apply these rules of presentation:

Rule 1: Make it simple. Wait, didn't I just say that? Yes, but make your presentation simple too. Use the smallest word, the simplest example, the shortest story that will make your point. You want your audience to experience communicating with you like an amusement park ride: Clear entry, simple story, a bit of tension, a quick conclusion, and immediate exit.[6]

Rule 2: Paint a picture. Build a metaphor or a diagram for the key point. A metaphor says, "It was like a [fill in the blank]" For instance: "The warehouse should look like a library: everything effortlessly in its place but easy to find." Where possible, draw your diagram by hand. It will keep you from the complexity that will put your audience to sleep. The three basic diagrams compare two things (A versus B, two-axis graph); three things (Venn diagram); or two things in two situations (double-axis chart). I am not drawn to diagrams, but I do them because others find them helpful.

Rule 3: Use a simple structure.

◊   Introduction: Why this topic now? Why does it matter?

◊   Three main points: State each in ten words or less.

◊   Picture: One diagram or example for each.

◊   Story: Tell a story that brings the diagram to life.

◊   Ask three questions about the story/diagram.

◊ Action statement: Here's what needs to happen next.

Close with a clear next step. To get there, you may need to slow down, clear up misunderstanding and fear with more questions, and invite next steps, in that order. Here's an example: Check the audience. Do they look dazed or ready to act? If dazed, say something like: "It looks like there's something else there." Wait sixty seconds. If it's time for actions, ask, "What should we do next?" In either case, listen and ask questions to understand. In both cases your questions are to bring the group to the same place if possible.

Just because you think you're clear about what's next doesn't mean that you're right or that your team understands clearly. Your process is to address both possible roadblocks to progress.

REWARD BEHAVIORS, NOT VICTORIES

Mastery is its own reward. It's a drug with infinite potential to continue to grow. It steps in front of winning and praise as a key driver of personal success. Folks who say winning is the only thing (some famous speakers) know that winners win because they obsess about mastery. The secret about mastery is that it's available every day, not just on game day. Doubt it? Reverse your picture and imagine winning without mastery. It's like ice cream (which I love): the pleasure peaks and then is gone.

Mastery is the slow drip that pulls us to do better than we imagined. Better yet, it's personal. Mastery doesn't require that you're better than everyone. Instead, it's a feeling of a small success, one after another. Mastery is built on a series of small successes, each one delivering the surge to the next one. One of the appeals of video games or card games is the combination of mastering a session or a hand and winning a game. The successive levels for video games are successive chances for mastery. The power of mastering the level is way past the power of mastering the whole video game.

Life is like that. Leadership could be like that. It's the task of the leader (teacher, coach) to break down the target into bites that lead to success. Those bites are opportunities to taste mastery, a little at a time. Mastery happens a little at a time, but pride and personal power surge forth at each step. It's that pride and personal power that fuel the hourly successes that your business and life are built on.

If you'll notice, you're surrounded with bite-size chances at mastery:

◊   Classes for an hour a day, every day.

◊   Hit 100 baseline shots.

◊   Shoot one clay pigeon at a time.

◊   Did we hit this hour's production target?

◊   Go one month without an accident by going accident-free today.

◊   Eat three meals a day.

◊ Do a math problem one step at a time.

◊ Practice four measures of the song until you play them exactly.

What if a company value was "To provide daily opportunities for mastery"?

Now compare what you already know about the power of the mastery experience to what you do as a leader—or worse, the structures that your company provides to enable mastery experience.

An intermission here, to clarify the value "To provide daily opportunities for mastery." If your reaction is that it's the employee's job instead of the company's job, I'd guess that your organization is a sitting duck for a competitor who consistently masters individual mastery. Yes, your customer offering, internal efficiencies, sales, and so forth must also be competitive.

Maybe it's time for a self-check. If things are working well, and you find yourself in the dual position of being the expense protector and the initiator, your leadership needs an outside examination. "Expense protector" means that your default on any new idea is no, unless outside evidence offers a compelling return. This stance kills chances for your people to enjoy individual mastery because they depend on your ideas and your agreement for it. They've learned not to suggest change that might need more thought or testing because you're a deflator instead of a mastery maker.

You might try this response to ideas that you aren't sure about:

1. What's your evidence that it will work as you say?

2. How would you assemble that evidence?

3. Let me help you see where that evidence might be.

You've shifted the conversation from deflator to chance for a little mastery: learning how to gather and evaluate evidence. Imagine the power of a team with that skill!

If you're the primary initiator, it's because you've trained your people to let you do it. Worse, you're likely doing well enough that the dragon of entropy is slipping into your organization, invisible so far. Entropy is the natural slowing of everything when there is no new energy to spin it back up.

The fastest way to strangle entropy is to tee up bits of potential mastery for everyone. They'll be so busy going for each little bit that things will improve, even though many ideas won't make it to execution. Just look in the mirror and accept the idling power of your people. That low buzz you hear is their engines waiting to be turned up. Mastery will do it ahead of any system of pay, bonus, or commission.

The Mastery Formula

The idling power of your people is missing unless you pull it in. In the absence of chances for personal mastery, most of your employees do their job to avoid criticism. You can check this too with a survey that asks each employee: "How do you know if you're doing a good job?"

Go ahead and try it. Make it convincingly confidential. Don't bury it in a longer list of questions; don't do it in public; don't include it in the annual review. Those all have baggage that will prevent either individual contemplation or honest answers. Just ask the one question and leave space for folks to write as much or as little as they want. Suggest that they ask their spouse or partner to help. Give them forty-eight hours to respond. If it's less, they may be unable to fit it in, delivering a pro forma answer that's biased by what they think you want to hear. If it's more, they won't see it as important, and many won't do it. See that someone chases down every employee, even part-timers. Every employee matters because you'll use this data in these ways:

1. To challenge your leadership team to rethink feedback and working with their people.

2. To revise your metrics and how they're explained and communicated.

3. To focus your executives on developing a culture that at least delivers these results:

   » Every employee knows how she's doing at least every month, if not daily.

   » Every leader has a simple system to report and record their people's performance.

   » Metrics provide real data that pretty much everyone agrees upon.

>> A burgeoning sense of priority about what folks work on.

>> Define your own result.

The data on the power of mastery makes actual leadership practice worth challenging because it's often off course. Sloppy or nonexistent performance evaluations, poor job design, few chances to share mastery . . . the list goes on.

There's another reason that parents insist, when talking to their kids about their sports games, that they just have a good time out there. Skip the part about "kids these days," prizes for all, and so forth. That's just so last century. No, the path to winning runs through a love of the game. It's that love that pulls us to try again. Yes, the hope of winning is fuel, but most of the life of an athlete is about practice, not the game. My grandson plays the trumpet. He's fourteen right now. He also plays whatever sport is in season, and more. Yes, there's a bit of drive to win a game or a prize, but every music lesson, every concert is a chance for a bit of the mastery reward. And in music as in sports, mastery is apparent through practice more than in a concert or a game.

What about victories? Aren't they important? Please tell me that your answer will be "Yes! They are chances for mastery!" It's just that there are so few games, so few annual reports, so few concerts, so few signed major customer contracts. Why not enjoy mastery every day?

MONEY IS NEVER A MOTIVATOR

The most ubiquitous data on leadership or management is that money is not a motivator, provided that basic compensation meets basic employee needs. And yet, leader after leader insists on reviewing their compensation program. I propose that pay structures are revised frequently because if feels like doing something for morale, motivation, performance, retention, employee satisfaction, and so forth. Take your pick. It's a way to avoid the tougher but more powerful ways to ignite excitement and motivation, as well as complaints about just about everything from leadership to the quality of the Internet.

Simplify the discussion. There are two kinds of pay: salary (with a bonus, if results enable it) or commission. There are two kinds of people: salary and commission. Match salary people with your salary plan and commission people with your commission plan. Check your rates in a well-regarded compensation survey; you'll have to pay for it or pay your HR firm to use theirs. Use a survey with job descriptions close enough to yours to show your people, and that matches your company size and geographic location. Adjust the amounts to the survey that fits you. Decide whether you want to pay your people in the top 10 percent, the top 25 percent, or the top 50 percent as a matter of policy.

Once you've matched your people to their pay pile (salary or commission), consider some details for special cases: super performers, high-potential new hires, and so on. Skip the drama about setting a precedent. Do the right thing, and be prepared to defend it to your board and your most cantankerous star employee.

Stop here: Money is still not a motivator, except for a few folks who prefer the risk of commission and who directly bring business to your company. Assistants, in-house salespeople, technicians, sales engineers, and all the hangers-on who want to get the commission without the risk do not get commission. Period. If they want it, let them earn their way to a position that pays a commission.

Do not give or sell minority shares of ownership in a privately held business. Pay performance bonuses in-stead. Minority ownership shares are deceptive on their face. Except for some form of annual profit-sharing, they are unlikely to deliver their value to an individual unless the company is sold. That contingency can be spelled out in a simple contract specifying either the dollar amount or percentage of sale proceeds that they will receive. Ownership should remain in the hands of owners, and the fewer the better. If ownership shares have enough value to be meaningful, most firms won't have the cash to pay them out except when the company is sold. A few folks mistake minority shares with something of value. They aren't.

Bonuses are best paid from an annual profit-sharing pot, limited by minimum earnings at the bottom and cash required for prudent operations at the top. Beyond that, pay it out. The simplest formula is to pay each per-son a percentage of the bonus pot that matches their salary/commission's share of total salary/commission. To earn more, they help the company earn more. Discretionary bonuses may also be paid, but out of the bonus pot if possible, to remain financially conservative. I recommend paying sales commission outside the bonus pot and consider them in cost of sales. Discretionary bonuses above commissions should also come out of the bonus pot.

There is a myth that departments or divisions should be paid based on their performance. If they depend on other parts of the company for sales, supply chain, finance, and so forth, their bonus should be inside the pot. They could not make the sale or deliver the product without others, and the distinction doesn't hold up under scrutiny.

Here's another pay secret: You can't give raises big enough to motivate with money. Think about it. Whether an employee salary is $150,000 a year or $300,000 a year, they likely are living close to their salary. A raise of 10 percent, toward the top of the range, in either case is nice but not revolutionary. The $150,000 employee gains an additional $15,000 before tax, or about $10,000 after tax. That's a down payment on the lease of a nice car, but not a home (even a vacation home). Even when you double it, the dilemma remains that it becomes supplementary salary, not breakthrough money. Breakthrough money is a fifty-foot sailboat, full college tuition for four years, a million-dollar house—add your example. Even worse, in most organizations there is an attempt at salary parity, which enables comparison of pay across the company to align somewhat with value delivered to the company. That usually produces pay ranges for positions, and raises are constrained by the pay schedule. The effect of that is to hold back part of a potential raise for the next raise period so there's room in the schedule for another raise. Translation: Pay itself is more about recognition than performance, especially on the upside. Poor performance can produce pay cuts, understandable to most folks. But great performance can produce modest raises, a "good" bonus within the bonus pool, and the possibility of promotion (mostly just recognition because, with a few exceptions at the very top of the company, the extra money won't cause an explosion).

Whew! Lots of baggage about pay and compensation. The real motivators? Here's a basic list that goes a long way toward the autonomy that most folks prefer, built upon a company norm that promotes maximum autonomy within required coordination:

◊ A boss who listens and is fair, respectful, and demanding (perfection not needed).

◊ A boss who is long on questions and short on orders.

◊ A job that provides the right mix of challenge and predictability (adapt the people to the job).

◊ A job frame that builds the fences that define the minimums and possibilities, such as:

» Goals for the smallest organizational units possible, in the shortest blocks of time.

» Up to four simple metrics to track performance daily and weekly.

» Annual performance goals across the company measured quarterly and annually.

» Frequent feedback (daily, if possible) about what's good and what needs to improve.

◊ Leaders who use the frame to provide frequent doses of encouragement and coaching.

◊ Leaders who see their jobs as mostly knocking down obstacles, cheering success, and salving the wounds of falling short.

◊ Leaders who involve their leaders in annual plans, goals, and measures by setting two levels:

» Total company: Planners include department leaders and high-potential junior folks.

» Each department or division: No more than three goals per department to enable intense focus, but goals aligned with company goals so all are pulling in the same direction.

◊ Special "skunk works" projects to exploit a major opportunity that current operations won't handle well.

This frame is like a baseball diamond. Once you know the rules of the game, it's easy for folks to play their position and enjoy it—and it's the enjoyment that pumps out the bursts of enthusiasm. Your question as a leader: How often do your people do each of these?

Chapter 8

It's Not What Happens, It's What You Do About It

Planning seldom asks, "Then what?" Yet it's precisely the "then what" capacity that gets a team across the finish line. There is always surprise. Power leadership seizes surprise as opportunity to create pride and greatness.

The power of surprise is well documented, from war to new products to death of a key player to real competition in your core market. From all the surprises documented around us, you'd expect that well-run businesses would employ surprise as a core competence and build in a defense against a surprise-rich world. We sometimes see one of these, but seldom both in the same company. It's so rare that you can immediately name the two or three firms that do both well. This, then, is an opportunity almost beyond bounds. Let's start after it.

Hope for the Best, Plan for the Worst

This phrase now has been turned inside out. The best companies say, "Plan for the best, and hope for even better." The problem with planning for the worst is defining what it looks like. In fact, there can be so many "worsts" that planning can't keep up. Instead, pour fuel on the plan, expecting to outrun the worst as it shows up.

Change what you plan for. Use two time horizons: known and possible. Excellence in the known is the launch pad to capitalize on surprise when it shows up.

The known plan is a low-risk adaptation of what works now: selling more to existing customers, recruiting new business in familiar markets, developing product line extensions, and so forth. This plan can be spelled out clearly enough to produce quarterly/monthly budgets, quarterly plans with daily KPIs, weekly reviews of KPIs, and core initiatives. This system, partly familiar, is still poorly executed in most companies that I see. We'll examine the two most common problems.

The Company Is the Leader

The leader built the business, has deep knowledge (of present staff, customers, processes, and opportunities), and closely controls all initiatives. This works well until it doesn't. That can happen because of growth, desire to sell the company, new leadership, and more. The core issue in that company is the leader—with his fingers in all the sockets. When too many things need to change at once, the leader falls short, often with delayed effect because many things appear to be alright.

The quickest diagnosis is to ask what will make things right. If the answer is more sales, it's time to shift to emergency mode. The business needs to expand its capacity to perform profitably and reliably and do it in many areas at once quickly. This requires a new structure that moves leadership out to new leaders with the communication systems, data systems, and sharper focus that success demands. Not big data, just data to run this business knowledgably. Competent leadership is even more scarce than adequate capital, although success takes both. The challenge is to allow change while things are still healthy.

An example (one of many) is a business (twenty-five-plus years old) run by its founder–leader. He said to me, "I've got to get my sons and son-in-law to grab this business and run it confidently and aggressively and do it now. We have a window to outrun our competition, but they don't have the confidence to step up and do it." What's more likely based upon my conversations with the owner is that he is unwilling (unable?) to hand over leadership, even in a planned way over time. He can't see that he's now in unfamiliar territory— empowering and teaching other leaders while he steps back—and he's blocking their growth.

It's like trying to teach a person to drive a car without letting them sit in the seat. They can watch forever, but until they hit the curb turning a corner they won't grasp what it takes. The trick is to let him drive and anticipate well enough to guide him away from lethal mistakes, while letting the other errors happen. We say to ourselves that it's okay for us to make mistakes because we learn from them, hiding how much we hate our mistakes, and then deny that learning to others.

Getting this leadership growth requires investing the time in goals, budgets, KPIs, initiatives (GBKI), and more.

Partial Shift from Leader to Leadership Team

Consider what happens when a leader has partly shifted to a leadership team with GBKI. The strength is in the framework defining the boundaries (GBKI). The vulnerability is the lack of discipline in evaluating progress daily or weekly, clearly identifying next steps, and seeking responsibility and accountability outside his or her office. The form is there, but the heart and the substance are missing where the power is: in the accountability and adaptiveness over time. The power in this system is that each employee knows what she needs to get done in the coming day or week, has a way to track success or problems, and can get competent help in a timely manner. The personal ownership of both task and quality captures the enthusiasm and willingness of employees who are in jobs that they love.

At this stage, firms can improve their operations and capacity for growth if they'll work seriously on accountability. Accountability isn't avoiding mistakes or owning them, it's owning processes that produce correct outcomes most of the time. It's a mix of anticipation, hard-headed plans, and tough follow-up that relies heavily on discipline and teaching instead of fear. That almost always requires leaders and workers who seek coaching and mentoring, who love to learn, and who mostly feel safe when things go wrong and they need to get help. It requires leaders who see their jobs as enabling others to succeed by seeing that these elements are in place:

◊ Leadership organizational structures that are up to the challenges of the month/year.

◊ Real-time evaluation/decision structures that demand high payback decisions.

◊ The right people in the right jobs with the right skills.

Even with all of these, a "gateway" leader who needs to initiate all high-value investments will be too slow, make too many mistakes, and drive away the gifted leaders who yearn for space to try their "stuff." With all of that, how does one convert an organization to one that excels when surprises occur? It's done by planning for the possible horizon. That is wordplay; it really means plan for surprises that you can't know in advance. How do you do that?

◊ Excel at GBKI—goals, budgets, KPIs, initiatives.

◊ Speed up introduction of new services or products, but demand excellence.

◊　Excel in finding weakness in new offerings and adapting to make them winners or withdrawing them from the market.

◊　Excel in using data to change operations. Instead of viewing each software installation as an excuse for poor performance, acknowledge that constant upgrades with excellence is a condition of doing business.

◊　Learn to lead when afraid! Robert Johansen, president of the Institute for the Future (a thirty-year-old Stanford Research Institute entity), posits that a VUCA world will demand leaders who can excel while overcome with fear. The uncertainty of a VUCA world means that much of the time leaders move into a dark room as they try to see what's needed in their organizations. All of us fear the dark when it likely includes danger, so that CEO fear is healthy realism. Some organizations are now using games to enhance top leaders' skill in performing while afraid, if not terrified. The games simulate life-altering challenge, forcing players to compete at full intensity while deeply afraid of losing! If you are competitive, you can see how the right game can put you there.

THE DIFFERENCE BETWEEN
STRATEGY AND TACTICS

There are two common frames for strategy: time and focus. But both are defined by the essential third: What do we want to be? Time and focus are tactical but lose their power without defining what we want to be. Tregoe and Zimmerman shift the focus to "driving force," which is the main way to decide future products and markets.[1] This shift away from operations is essential to avoid the common error of increasing last year by 5 percent and calling it a strategic plan. It is neither. Pull back a minute to reestablish that a business is first about the scope of its products (services) and markets. It is only then about the business model, sales, production, and so forth.

Even more, the driving force is a necessary limit on all elements of the business, providing a lens to clarify which roads to follow, and which to ignore. The concept is slippery, but worth the capture. Driving force is the single concept that captures the unique strength of the company, helping to shed appealing ideas that are less likely to come to fruition. Tregoe and Zimmerman offer a collection of driving forces that can clarify the area that must excel for the business to succeed. It doesn't exclude others but demands that it be protected and exploited with all available vigor if success is a serious goal. These examples of driving force can be useful to help you frame your own, if you clarify to all employees their central role in your present and future success. Here are Tregoe and Zimmerman's driving forces, with examples:[2]

STRATEGIC AREA (DRIVING FORCE)	EXAMPLE
Products offered	Ford, Bank of America
Market needs	Gillette, Merrill Lynch
Technology	DuPont, US Center for Disease Control
Production capability	US Steel, International Paper
Method of sale	Franklin Mint, Amazon
Method of distribution	MacDonald's, Comcast
Natural resources	Shell Oil, DeBeers Consolidated Mines
Return/profit (Return/profit determine scope of markets and products)	BlackRock, Bain Capital

The summary is that a single driving force is a powerful frame for future company decisions, and therefore worth the effort to develop. It comes alive as a strategy, and tactics are developed to pursue it. The question "What do we want to be?" can be explained to frame every other decision, financial, tactical, hiring, expansion, choice of industry, and more.

The *time* approach limits strategy to a future period, usually three or five years. It uses both budgets (annual budgets for three or five years) and broad action plans to accomplish budget targets. Tactics are then the specific actions within each company department to execute the current year's portion of the three-to-five-year strategy.

The *focus* strategy considers broader lines of business as possibilities, such as transportation or resource recovery (mining, oil drilling, etc.). These broader possibilities are then refined within estimates of depth of opportunity, strength of competition, and the amount of capital and expertise the firm must have to be number two or number one in that business domain. Those resource estimates help to select among equally attainable strategic paths, weighting time and probability of success to refine the strategic direction. That direction then devolves into one-year and three-year tactical budgets and plans, driving related one-year department tactical plans.

The three-point perspective of Leilani Schweizer pulls actionable opportunities into the spotlight faster and with less wasted motion. Schweitzer first tried every way she could think of to change the medical system that mistakenly killed her twenty-month-old son. Finally, applying a design technique from her courses at Montana State University, she helped reduce medical errors by creating a three-dimensional perspective on medical care through the eyes of the three groups at the center of medical care: physicians, nurses, and patients. "This process bends space and time, allowing us to see an object from three perspectives with a single drawing. We need to see multiple views—from doctors, nurses, patients, administrators, and volunteers—at one time." Only then, she said, will health-care providers understand problems fully enough to "find true, long-term solutions."[3]

For your business, replace SWOT by creating a Schweitzer three-dimensional strategy perspective: Ask departments to look through the lens of opportunity and weakness at customers, competitors, and the future to produce real target products or services. It is most manageable with a two-to-three-year target, provided the contributors include senior executives and department leaders in the firm. Draft perspectives can benefit from review by a board of directors, if it has the strategic breadth to consider those possibilities. That's a nice way of saying that if your board is your dad, your lawyer, and your accountant, their contribution will focus mostly on limits rather than possibilities. At this stage, the wisdom should be about possibilities, leaving to management the task of parsing possibilities and their respective return and risk.

Tactics at their best combine operations targets with selected initiatives. Operations targets emphasize efficiency, quality, and customer service. Initiatives drive selected improvements in existing operations or launch of new products or services. Their management requires a different rhythm of measures and adjustments, as well as close involvement of different levels of management.

Line teams are best equipped to find and implement operations efficiencies, pulling in technical help to frame problems at the right breadth and offer more technical solutions when needed.

The problem with becoming an efficiency-only company is, as one wag said, that you can't cut your way to growth. The real problem is near-term emphasis. Cutting expenses or boosting efficiencies is enormously rewarding, easy to measure, and easy to award recognition to folks who can see their contribution.

The alternative is to deliver new products or services while maintaining the excitement about efficiency. New anything is fuzzy, uncertain, hard to defend, and essential to health. The most courageous leaders at every level are those who have the grit (see book with the same name by Angela Duckworth) to keep at both and do it in public.

A simple diagnostic: What's new in this year's plan? If the "new" launches more than three years out, you've got challenges of focus and execution. Three years out frequently translates to "never."

Launch of new products or services builds upon special development efforts by cross-functional teams that refine the concept of an offering to assure its customer appeal, and then refine its consistent production within the company. It sounds simple and fails often enough to justify this warning: New offerings take twice the money and three times the talent and time, and still frequently fall flat. Success comes from the inspired ("emotional") drive of key lower-level leaders, not lofty speeches from the CEO.

LEADING THROUGH AMBIGUITY

The successful executive inbox looks like Times Square on steroids, closing at hyper speed. The urgency hides the ambiguity of impact and cost. Instead, success is the continuing skill to determine where to place the biggest resources: people, money, and time. The fog of ambiguity blocks the view past the decision room, offering wisps of insight into the future.

Deploying resources requires sizing up the future as it speeds into view and making choices about deploying those resources. Ambiguity is the inevitable partner of successful leaders. That ambiguity can be moderated with time, data, and analysis, but the fundamental uncertainty of launching into the dark room of the future remains. That uncertainty is both about the future situation outside the company, and the performance of the company as it enters the dark room. The challenge is

The Decision Fog

Now   DECISION ARENA   Then

to balance opportunity with company capability, and then determine whether the risk justifies an investment. That sounds cerebral, reeking of quiet rooms full of brilliance and insights. In fact, it's a sequence of rooms of messy ideas, incomplete analysis, personal bias, and the ticking clock of opportunity escaping. The unspoken promise of clear decisions powered by firm alternatives just doesn't exist. The successful move forward when they have 60 percent information. Waiting bleeds opportunity dry.

So, if all is fuzzy, what are some guideposts?

◊ Press to see all opportunities that you might exploit.

◊ Upside: Roughly sort payback and feasibility, quickly. (Could we do it? If so, what do we get?)

◊ Downside: Compare risk and payback. (Does the payback justify the risk?)

◊ What's the expected value of success versus the cost?

The Secret of Expected Value (EV)

Expected value is a simple way to sort options based upon risk and payback. The beauty of the approach is that rough estimates can yield excellent results. How can that be? EV works on "coarse decisions," where the choice is about exactly where to invest resources to refine a specific approach. It lets the user engage more options faster, without the "engineer's dilemma": The engineer–thinker wants to know how something will be done before committing to do it. The problem is that this reasonable-sounding approach deletes options that might be realized with the right investment in the "how." It's also a way to tone down the ecstasy of a fabulous solution that's beyond unlikely but offers magical returns. High-potential returns sometimes have a way of fogging the reason. Table 8.1 displays an example of EV.

Table 8.1 Example of Expected Value (EV)

ESTIMATED RETURN/ YEAR	PROBABILITY OF SUCCESS	EV
$500,000	.20 (2 out of 10)	$100,000
$500,000	.30 (3 out of 10)	$150,000
$300,000	.70 (7 out of 10)	$210,000

(EV is the percent likelihood of success multiplied by the payback minus the cost; return on investment is EV divided by cost, as a percent.)

The expected value takes in the possibility of failure but not the cost of it. The cost of failure may be the first measure. It's not the cost of trying, but rather the cost of the lost opportunity (opportunity cost), measured in these dimensions:

◊   Lost profit on lost sales.

◊   Lost opportunity for further revenue.

◊   Lost opportunity for improved efficiency at higher volume.

◊ Opening the door to strengthen a competitor who may then seek your existing business.

Opportunity cost can be calculated like expected value, and the EV benefit can be compared to the EV cost for a sharper picture into the future.

◊ Formula: Is the expected value enough greater than the opportunity cost to justify action?

◊ What is our capacity to recover if the investment delivers far less than planned?

This process can be cut to shorthand to surface only opportunities worthy of attention. Data will not remove the ambiguity, however, because ambiguity holds the opportunity to earn significant returns. Ambiguity is an unsolved problem. The ones who solve it well may— *may*—reap a reward.

The problems:

◊ The reward may be out of reach.

◊ The cost damages cash capacity.

◊ The diversion damages existing customer service and product quality.

◊ The diversion removes key employees who return to the main business too late to bring it back to health.

The first ambiguity: Should we pursue this opportunity? The second ambiguity: Can our teams execute this plan well enough to hit our goals?

Moving folks who excel in the established company to the new entity sounds appealing, but it's a double risk: They are removed from making the money that keeps the business going, and they may need the historic structure, history, and undocumented ways of doing things to be successful. It's one thing to lead an established business, even when it needs improvement. It's quite another to frame for the first time the norms, processes, measures, revenue building, margin and inventory management, and customer service systems that a successful new business requires. A common error is to understate the time and mistakes that building a new entity takes, basing that on the time it would take the existing business to accomplish these things. And the middle ground doesn't work (keep the best folks in their current jobs and ask them to produce the future).

Ambiguity extends beyond the yes/no decision to performance in the new entity. Even if all of the above is on the mark, execution over time can erode profit and will, leaving an organization tired of the task.

All of this explains why so few companies produce entirely new products and services. The swoon for growth ignores these realities, as though brains and discipline will deliver success. They seldom do. The dirty secret of venture capitalist investors is that most of their investments fail. Most. They presumably are best equipped to find the winners and guide them to success, but what of the rest of us?

For some folks, the fascination of risk and the possibility of great reward are enough to chase breakthrough businesses. For most of us, incremental growth is enough. The problem is that our competition is in the same place, so the game goes not to the inventor of the new concept but to those who execute beautifully. Apple and Microsoft are examples.

The single best way to cut the paralysis of ambiguity is relentless focus on delivering excellence. Ambiguity lives in every untried idea, even those about better execution. In fact, dramatically better execution wins most races today. The scandal of exploding auto airbags is evidence of that because the scandal is that the airbags were faulty, not that they exploded. Their explosions were dramatic and terrible, but cars are now routinely complex and virtually error-proof. That routine is the result of years of intense focus on execution.

OPPORTUNISM AND INNOVATION

Innovation happens because people set out to find a better way. There are always two parts to the innovation process: think it up and make it work in the world.

Part A (Think it up) Innovation possibility formula:
Who finds it? + What's the appeal?

Part B (Make it work) Survival test:
Who wants it? + What do they think they will be buying?

Part C Business model:
How likely is profitable volume? When?

Until you're excited about *A*, skip *B* and *C*. The recycling bins are full of weak ideas that someone hoped would rise from the dead as they were massaged into viable products.

The legendary product development focus of 3M is simple: Give people who want it some time to come up with something they could be passionate about. Then use the passion to do the hard work of birthing (or killing) a new product, with a little money to help.

Why not turn Silicon Valley inside out? Instead of leadership guilt about data bloat (*there must be something we can do with the data*), why not look away from the computer? Why not use IT to help deliver something that people really want? Lose the next computer toy and switch your lens to the people that you live with, work with, sell to, and buy from.

Salt and Straw is a fabulously successful chain of West Coast ice cream stores. They have married the product innovation of Ben & Jerry's with a happy environment of upbeat music full of smiling folks offering spoons of flavors you'd never try without a sample

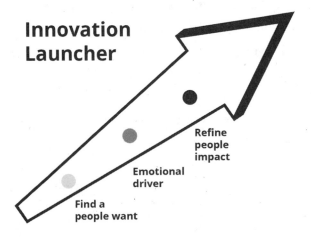

Innovation Launcher

Refine people impact

Emotional driver

Find a people want

(coconut and bee pollen?). And yes, there's a people story behind each flavor: "Sebastian Cisneros began as a chocolatier but started sourcing and roasting beans from his native Ecuador to make his own flavors of chocolate. To honor his new Abeja bar, we make a bee pollen and baked milk custard ice cream ribboned with dark chocolate fudge."[4] The stores are places where people want to go, unlike the dreary, dirty, sterile chain stores that they compete with. The power in this innovation is in the happy people and the happy store. The rest is good but not remarkable. The innovation is that it's a happy place that happens to sell ice cream. The lines are out the door daily, even in winter. People will pay a lot to be instantly happy, especially if there's no hangover. *That* is the innovation—and you get ice cream.

Turn the usual new product process on its head. Ask people questions first:

1. What would people love to change (start or stop)?

2. What do people hate about their work, their product, their process?

3. What do people like to do around here?

4. What would customers dearly like to make disappear?

Refine these like gold: Cook ideas down until their people appeal is clear. (Of course, there are improvements that improve profit, but the ones that last are the ones that people learn to love.) The basic principle is to focus on the ideas, not on the process of evaluation, trial, adjustment, and so forth. Those are needed, but if the ideas are lousy, they don't matter. Further, if each good idea has a patron who will kill to make it successful, the test and growth periods are more likely to pay off.

Pick your wildly successful product idea: Facebook? Started by college guys who wanted a quick reference of girls in their school—a hormone-driven product that cost nothing but time on the computer. It got off the ground because of passionate sponsorship. Subsequent iterations had many drivers, but the power is in the original basic concept.

Let's make this even simpler. Sort your search for ideas driven by emotion. You know, love, hate, fear, aversion, embarrassment, frustration—you add to the list. In fact, go back to the numbered items on page 183. Read them quickly, and stop when one of them provokes an emotion in you.

Your personal refining process:

◊   What's that about, in you?

◊   Is it something that other people might click with?

◊   What would boost the power of its appeal?

Now invite other folks into the game—people who want to have fun with a new idea. Ask them to go through the same processes in the next twenty-four hours. That will provide a basket of ideas that might have some people power that's bigger than you imagine.

People who work with machines all day have all kinds of feelings about their machines and their workdays. When I worked in a trash hauling company, I was amazed to learn that drivers timed themselves all day, with critical time points on each route. The payoff was finishing early to go do something else they liked to do. When we proved that there was no safety or service risk (owner's concerns), drivers could go home when they were done, and in less than a month we revised their routes to be more efficient. That saved enough truck hours so that we could avoid buying another truck to service additional yard debris (mandated by the city). All were happy: owner, drivers, customers, city. In this case, the passion was avoiding fake work and getting some free time that they wanted.

What about opportunism? Opportunism is a suggestion box writ large—huge, in fact. By the way, if you're successful with a suggestion box for eighteen months or more, please call me immediately. I'd like to know how you did it because you'll be the first that I've met. A suggestion box is opportunism with nobody home, and there's no cheering squad to light up the person with the idea. It works at first, but then the combination of dreadful ideas and employee anger at rewards that are either insufficient or irrelevant pretty much grinds the program away. Just don't do it.

Instead, how about listening? Wait! Before you roll your eyes, try this: Schedule at least one hour a week to walk around and listen to a few folks. Ask the next question after they've answered your first one. The next question? Something like one of these:

◊ Why now?

◊ How is that different from what we're doing?

◊ I'm not sure I understand. Could you explain that a bit more?

These discussions will be idea starters for some improvements, or maybe door-busters, if you'll listen, probe, and act interested. It's really in there, but it needs to be coaxed out like coaxing a cat to a new dish of food (or a dog, if you're not a cat person. Neither am I.).

Here's a listening tip from one of the best: Oprah Winfrey. If she's become a billionaire by doing this, maybe she's worth a listen. In this scenario, she is listening to folks in a small group equally divided between Trump supporters and Trump non-supporters. Sitting next to a Trump supporter: "I could feel him tense up. I decided not to take on his tension, but to do the opposite, which was to lean in. . . . Every time I feel him bristle, I turn and say, 'Tell me what you think, what do you say about that?' That is how you hear people."

"It's her superpower," says Reese Witherspoon. "She really listens, and *she is genuinely interested* [emphasis added]."[5]

This is a top payoff to you, if you'll decide to master it. It's about attending to the other person, despite your own discomfort. Your challenge as a leader is to listen with genuine interest, in two areas at once: the people and the content of what they are saying. Most of us are trained to value the content first, and it shows. The problem is that your success depends on those people even more than on their ideas. If you doubt it, then *you* go do their job.

Chapter 9

The Talent Quest

Talent is the engine of the enterprise. More than the right seat on the bus, it is matching real output with company needs in real time. Change now requires broadly skilled individuals playing on broadly skilled teams to surf the tsunami of change that swirls about us even now.

Before you assume that "talent" is something that only big firms do, consider this: The *Wall Street Journal* reported on January 31, 2018, that Amazon, JPMorgan Chase, and Berkshire Hathaway "plan to form a company to reduce their workers' health costs."[1] Instead of emphasizing the technical approaches one would expect from such firms, Berkshire chairman Warren Buffett said they believe "putting our collective resources behind the country's best talent" can deliver on such a promise. Look again. One of the nation's stellar collections of technical expertise is talking about talent first! Draw your own conclusions, but if folks who can buy whatever they want are talking first about talent, there must be something there, and of course there is.

RECRUITING TALENT

Who does the organization appeal to? Much is made of the appeal of organizational culture to attract the kinds of people who will power its success. It may be argued that there are two kinds of organizational appeal:

◊ Type 1: The opportunity to grow and be promoted to positions with more power, influence, and money.

◊ Type 2: The opportunity to enjoy meaningful work with peers who value each other, in settings that provide the autonomy, mastery, and purpose that build meaning.

These appeals broadly define the hopes and expectations of two types of employees. One gladly seeks the risk and discomfort of moving to a new position before thoroughly mastering the old. She or he thrives on change and increasing responsibility, and in fact, measures success by the speed of those changes. The bent toward change, growth, and promotion provides the fuel for the constant improvement that marks most industries today. These employees are fewer in most firms, but essential to survival.

The other employees are the folks who get most of the actual "work" done. They value more predictability and safety, will devote years to mastering their skills, and will be drawn to organizations that recognize their contributions regularly. Their ability to find other jobs can be more limited because their need for security makes changing jobs uncomfortable.

Cy Green, legendary former president of billion-dollar retailer Fred Meyer, explained these differences to me in a conversation that began like this: "If there's a problem with a store employee, I'll likely take their side." Paraphrasing, he continued, you don't need the protection, you're willing to take career risks, and you have the resilience to bounce back. They will trade new situations for the safety and familiarity of work that they know they can do well. They often can't protect themselves very well, so I'll be happy to do that. We need both of you.

Recruiting is wrongly defined as searching for the "right" kinds of talent, when it really is about what is needed along a time continuum from now into an uncertain future. These categories of positions need to be made explicit in job discussions, if not in position descriptions. Also, relying on past job descriptions to define the next position is seldom adequate because it looks to the known past more than the possible future.

A better recruiting question: What will this position need to deliver in the next three years? A job description starting from that question has a better chance of delivering a successful employee to almost any position.

The debate about whether to fill the position or promote from inside is over. The recruiting sequence for success is:

◊   Define the position needed in the coming three years.

◊   Prepare for an external candidate search.

◊   Use search criteria to evaluate internal candidates.

◊   Seek outside candidates when no adequate internal candidate is found.

A new twist: The appeal of company culture is personal, but it extends beyond the employee setting, and rightly so. This culture has expanded outside organizations to their locations and the life that such a location offers. Urban studies expert Richard Florida (*The Rise of the Creative Class*) documents in exhaustive detail a relatively new and powerful phenomenon: It is common now for workers to choose a job because of its location. That's the reverse of patterns that have existed since the American Civil War (1860) when workers

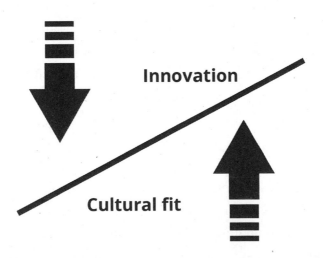

Innovation

Cultural fit

moved where the jobs were. The underground railroad provided a path, not just to escape slavery, but to find jobs and the income that provided for the kind of life that those folks sought.

Today, more than even five years ago, prospective employees ask questions like these:

◊ What kinds of people work there?

◊ What's important to folks who work there now?

◊ What kind of place is it located in?

Successful recruiting will have prepared answers to these questions that anticipate the preferences of desirable employees, not only about job specifics, but also about these softer characteristics.

New data from Stanford Graduate School of Business suggests that adaptability may be as important as cultural fit over time at a firm. Amir Goldberg of Stanford and three coauthors reviewed more than ten million internal emails from a technology firm over five years, tracking cultural fit with linguistic analysis: "Language use is intrinsically related to how individuals fit, or fail to fit, within social environments," and, "what predicts who will stay . . . leave . . . [or] be fired is . . . the degree to which they adapt," Goldberg says.[2] "Adaptability means working effectively within multiple departments, locations, and company units over time."[3]

There is always the challenge of balancing cultural fit with innovative drive, but the best answer seems to be the ability to shape the innovation to enable the culture to embrace it well.

Increasingly, I see leaders who are reluctant to move aside employees in critical positions when they are no longer able to perform as needed. Instead of demanding excellence from each of their people, especially leaders, a combination of avoiding pain and wishful thinking perpetuates problem performance. The cost to company performance is high, but that pales beside the damage to the morale of other employees and equally to the struggling employee. Usually, the failing employee knows they are falling short well before the boss is ready to talk about it, producing fear and destroying the self-confidence that's essential in any position and to living a life with some meaning.

Here is a way to approach such a problem situation with these questions, talking privately with the employee and listening especially carefully:

◊   How are things going?

◊   It seems like things are a bit of a struggle right now.

◊   How is it for you?

◊   Would you like to consider a different position that would be more comfortable for you?

◊   We can help you find it, write a letter of recommendation listing your considerable skills, and support your job interviews inside or outside the company.

◊   Would you like to consider that?

That discussion has produced tears, relief, and gratitude, sometimes in just a few days. Recruiting is mischaracterized as a search process. It's mostly not, but instead it is about clarity and agreement among key leaders about exactly why the position is needed, what it should contribute, and then what the core attributes of the employee might be. Almost always it's better to hire for attitude than for experience, even when there is a core of technical skill needed. After all, your most skilled people learned what they know; they weren't born with it. If they can learn, so can a new person, and a proven learner has much higher value now and in the future.

SUSTAINING AND DEVELOPING TALENT

Sustaining and developing talent demand similar activities. Both thrive with simple, "on the ground" programs, rather than sweeping promises. Often the headset of top leaders is a problem, with beliefs like these (followed by a rebuttal):

◊ *What we have is working fine.* Tomorrow will be different, and if our incumbent is just keeping up now, he'll drown in the flood of the future.

◊ *The risks of bringing in a new person are too high for us.* Not developing people for our future is a bigger risk than the risk of a hiring failure.

◊ *We aren't good at training or developing peo-ple.* Begin to learn by finding a leader who is good at it and tasking her to teach others.

◊ *We need the right person right now.* If you're saying this, you're already too late. Patch together temporary operations support until you can hire the right person.

◊ *I don't see a person in the company who can fulfill the position.* Shift your focus to aptitude and drive instead of skills and experience.

◊ *Hiring is much too expensive.* If you're con-sidering hiring, the need is likely deeper and more acute than you realize, and the comfort of waiting will be replaced with declining results. Which heartache do you prefer?

In my work coaching senior executives, a surpris-ingly pervasive problem is unwillingness to delegate and demand performance from key reports.

The monkey on your back is a metaphor for taking on a project. Many people will try to hand the monkey to their boss ("How do I do this?"), and their boss com-pounds the error by taking the project (monkey). That reinforces these destructive messages in both people:

◊ I'm better at this than you are.

◊ It will take you too long to learn to do it.

◊ We can't afford to risk this project on someone like you.

◊ It's faster to do it myself.

Is the damage worse to the leader or the subordinate? It's a tie of bad news. The leader retrenches into familiar work instead of doing the less familiar but higher impact work that his job calls for. The subordinate hears denial of confidence in him, a narrowing of his responsibility to familiar work, and reduced chance of growth in skill or responsibility in this position. The ensuing weak performance is disastrous to the leader's results and career promise. The subordinate may recover faster, if she promptly moves to another leader and lets go of the bad experience.

Delegation can create a faith gap, where the leader lets go and waits to see if the employee picks up the ball well enough and soon enough. The blind spot seems to defy logic. If a leader has four direct reports of adequate competence, he can delegate and monitor the performance of all four in much less time than doing it himself. Instead, he will micromanage parts of projects to "be sure that things are being done well"—code for doing it his way. This behavior drives away top people and limits the performance of the team and the leader. It's logically crazy, but it's driven by feelings, not logic.

Consider levers: Bulldozers, tanks, and other vehicles on tracks steer with a pair of levers that control the speed and direction of each track. Moving the levers works like a steering wheel on steroids, multiplying the driver's power. A leader's people are like those levers. They are the direct link to the work that needs to be done and to how and when it's done. Yet this logical picture sweeps past many leaders who are in love with their task skills.

A CEO of a midsize software business was a brilliant sales leader. Sadly, when his very competent chief revenue officer tried to review a plan with him, the leader would pick up his pen to scrawl new ideas and make changes to the CRO's excellent plan. The differences in approach weren't enough to justify the disconnect with one of the most critical leaders in the company. He went away fuming and disheartened, depending on others to restore his confidence and excitement about his work (which was indeed exciting in every good sense). It took months of work and discussion to repair the breach in the relationship from the CRO's side.

The problem with recognizing poor performance isn't what to do about it, it's calling it out as a problem that needs attention. The potential upset with another person, and perhaps a gap in the leadership roster, will pull the problem to the B pile for another day. The answer for a leader is to ask the subordinate leader directly about performance data. That moves the discussion to the data and then to possible next steps, which boil down to train or replace. When the subordinate leader repeats this error, it's time for focused coaching on the topic. "Focused" often means going to an outside coach whose focus can prompt real change.

My wife repots her orchids after they bloom. They return with a rush of new blooms, often bigger and better than before. Who needs repotting in your organization? Repotting can range from a change in subordinate to a gain or loss of a responsibility to a challenge to develop a subordinate to be ready for the next position.

Mentorship is another powerful concept that's misunderstood. It can be useful to encourage diversity or to help other younger executives begin to understand how to be "seen" and appreciated by top leadership in a company, but that's not it's primary power for retaining and training people. As Sheryl Sandberg, Facebook COO and author of *Lean In,* says, "So shift your thinking from 'If I get a mentor, I'll excel' to 'If I excel, I will get a mentor.'"[4] People in any organization who do well for the goals of the organization will be noticed by others. That opens the door to working on a project or a presentation with a potential mentee or mentor.

Robust mentorship can provide frequent recognition and challenge to folks whose daily and weekly work may not provide much of either. Recognition and challenge with support are essential for building morale and hope—and those are foundations for great performance.

The other secret of a robust mentorship program, besides faster and deeper development of subordinates, is the leadership development available to mentors. It comes in small enough bites to make it useful. Leadership is significantly about influencing other people, and mentorship is the ideal way to test new skills with low risk and prompt feedback. Yes, mentorship is a partnership if it's to be successful. If either partner decides that the wisdom resides in them, it's game over and time to move on.

Carlos Slim, head of Mexico's largest telecom, is one of the world's wealthiest men. His personal wealth has recently dropped 20 percent since AT&T has entered the Mexican market. Ironically, twenty years ago he taught (mentored) the business to employee Randall Stephenson, now CEO of AT&T. Mentorship power, indeed![5]

The basic prescription has two parts:

1. Spend more time and money in recognition than compensation.

2. Teach delegation as an active requirement of leadership.

Recognition tops every study on motivation I've ever seen (provided basic compensation is fair). Make the skillful practice of recognition as vital as making the numbers for every employee. Stop the speeches and make active recognition a daily requirement of employment. If you truly don't know how, ask a first-grade teacher how he does it. Better yet, watch a class and see it live. It's mostly a habit with a tiny bit of skill.

The "how" of delegation is more particular, but the leadership directive is to bring it alive. Every person who supervises another person should be able to answer this question at any time: What have you delegated today? Here's a simple delegation framework that works for almost anyone. Skip a step at your peril.

THE DELEGATION FRAMEWORK

1. Name the task.

2. Name the leader.

3. Hand over the entire task to a person or a pair.

4. Check for understanding: "What will you do?"

5. Ask how they will measure progress.

6. Ask what resource (if any) they will need.

7. Ask for a first report back date (e.g., "Let me know Friday how it's coming.").

8. Ask for a completion or substantial progress date (e.g., "When do you think you'll finish?").

9. Be available to help. If there's silence for a week, ask if help is needed.

10. After they've hit some of the targets, invite a brief update to the management team. (Optional)

SHARE THE TALENT:
EMPLOYEES HELP EACH OTHER TO GROW

Sharing talent is not exclusively an HR function. It belongs to line management everywhere as they are the ones always asking for more people, better people, or more machines. Most people love to be recognized, and being asked to help is a high compliment—so ask. But ask for help instead of assigning a task: "Would you help me sort out this information?"

Model Two-Way Communication

Even though top leaders are regularly quoted as saying, "I learn more from my people than they learn from me," most discussion about communication focuses on a single direction, usually down (from leaders to subordinates). Up is better than just down, but two-way communication is even better.

The four stages of communication:

1. None: "You know what to do."

2. Down: "I know what you should do."

3. Up: "Here are ways to improve."

4. Two-way: "Let's attack it together."

5. What's a leader to do?

   » Institutionalize: Make it "something we do here."

   » Check: Ask, "What ideas have you gotten from your people this week?"

   » Recognize: At every all-hands meeting, recognize one pair that's done it.

   » Include outside employees in management team meetings as observers.

More Simple Tools

These tools work if you rise from your chair and do them.

One that's very effective is regular skip-level visits by leaders. The rules:

1. Go see folks who work at least one level below your direct reports.

2. Ask them up to three questions:

   » What are you proud of?

   » What makes your job hard?

   » Who helps you?

3. Take brief notes.

4. Listen. Ask questions only to help you understand.

5. Offer no direction.

6. Find one good thing they've done and praise them on the spot.

7. Practicing one-minute praising is another effective technique. It's simple, but details are everything:

   » Praise immediately.

   » Stop and face the person; a drive-by doesn't work.

   » Look into their eyes, and see if you can see who's in there.

   » Praise a specific act. Name it.

   » Admit how it makes you feel: pleased, relieved, proud, etc.

   » Pause. Count to five to let it sink in.

   » Thank them.

   » Ask them to keep doing it.

   » Move on. Don't dilute the moment with any comment.[6]

The excuse "I don't praise much" exists in many forms. Skip the psychobabble about why, and just make it a job requirement. Here's how:

◊ Approach it like any other high-value team responsibility.

◊ Make it an annual goal in your planning session.

◊ Quantify what a good job looks like (e.g., five a week, one a day, etc.).

◊ Provide brief hands-on practice for every leader.

◊ Require an action tally (how many) as part of the agenda for every one-on-one.

◊ Post weekly results by department, perhaps number of praisings as a percentage of number of employees.

◊ Recognize praising expertise in all-hands meetings.

◊ You get the idea. Instead of a limp, "You all know this is important," raise it to the level of a major initiative.

For those who demand an ROI, explain that the best research shows that recognition, especially public recognition, ranks way ahead of pay and bonus for motivation. The exception may be salespeople, but because the requirement for success is always fair pay as a hygiene factor, simply pay salespeople fairly and add praise on top, like the cherry on a hot fudge sundae. Of all people, salespeople are generally most motivated by praise and recognition, so what's to lose?

In short, the free investment of regular praise will boost the numbers. We're awash in studies, so instead of reciting another one, I dare you to find a reputable study that proves that money beats recognition. There will be a prize—perhaps recognition on LinkedIn.

For a simple recognition booster, tie the praise to a specific impact on the business, such as customer service, quality, cost, pricing, or efficiency. Most employees are deeply invested in the place where they work, and that investment will boost the power of recognition.

Robert MacLellan, founder of the remarkably successful Pacific Coast Restaurants, will enumerate "free" actions by restaurant staff that played a significant part in their success. For example, a chef may not yell at a server, ever. There is one chance, and then the chef leaves. Why? Who wants an upset server at your table when you hope to enjoy a meal?

Or consider the bartender story as told by Robert MacLellan (a bit longer, but worth it). Picture yourself in the far corner of a bar just as happy hour starts. A man walks in, sits at the end of the bar. Bartender walks over, smiles, asks four questions, listening between each one: "Where are you from? What do you do? What brings you to town? What are you drinking?" Soon a woman walk in, sits at the bar (you guessed it) as far away from the man as possible. (Robert's translation: If an unaccompanied man sits down in a bar next to an unaccompanied woman, or vice versa, there is immediate tension and discomfort, usually in both folks . . . unless there are no other seats available.) Bartender repeats the same questions with the woman. After a bit, the bartender walks over to woman, picks up her drink, starts moving toward the man, saying, "There's someone I'd like you to meet." Woman obliges, bartender seats her next to the man, introduces them to each other by name, where they're from, what they do, and why they're in town. They start talking. Now, it's not at all what you think. There's no hanky-panky. Instead, the customer experience is that it's a friendly, safe, pleasant place. The bartender repeats with other customers. After some weeks, people ring the bar four deep. They love coming there to talk with their friends! A group that met at the bar develops and starts a tradition of traveling together!

What's the point? Try treating your people, all your people, as folks that you like and admire (even if you must pretend). Pause occasionally and listen to them. Just listen, nod, smile, and look for reasons to connect with them or like them. That's all. That's a rich recognition that's free and makes a huge difference in their day-to-day work at your company.

Try Forced Growth

My early training included moving to a new assignment well before I thought I'd mastered the current one. Admittedly, I love a challenge, but the result was high-speed learning, a regular challenge, and pride in what we accomplished. I was to design and install a bakery concept in a major Chicago food retailer that would "be as good as the best Chicago bakeries, and break even." That was the assignment. As a kid from Portland, Oregon, I had never encountered Danish dough, let alone artisanal bread or water injection ovens. The learning was a doorbuster for the rest of my life: I could help people with deep expertise apply themselves to a larger project and do it successfully. We designed and then built twenty-nine bakeries before I moved on— and they were magnificent! I'm still proud of what we accomplished, and there was no bonus or special compensation, except my pride in our team and our bakeries, which survives years since!

EVERY EMPLOYEE AN OWNER

One of the company owners that I worked with for several years periodically said, "This would be great if it weren't for the people!" Now, he likes people a little at a time, but he hates confrontation or disagreement. More accurately, he feels flummoxed when he runs into it, doesn't know what to do next, and worse, doesn't know how to prevent it, so he runs away from it. His answer regularly was, "If everyone just acted like an owner!" I think he missed the irony, because he's the owner.

The real point is about motivation and behavior, however. And here's the fantasy, summarized: If I could just inject motivation into people, things would work better (and smoother). This is naïve.

There is no tool, system, practice, culture, or magic that will motivate people; and those who are not owners will not be motivated like an owner—even broader ownership. That's like saying that people should act like astronauts. The problem is that most people will never be in a space station, and they won't be owners of the place where they work.

How to motivate employees? Here's a starter list:

Pay for the job, with minor adjustments for performance and skill. Pay them at least market rates (salary) and provide for regular reviews to see that their pay links to market pay. Don't pay a high-potential person for their future contribution, except in the initial hire. Make it clear that compensation increases come from their contribution to the success of the business. And change the dialogue from pay to compensation so their bonus and benefits are included. It's obvious to your accountant but not to most employees because what they regularly see is the cash part of their paycheck.

Allocate bonuses by the ratio of individual salary to total salary dollars. Develop a company-wide profit sharing system that allocates a percentage of company profit to the company profit pool each year, and avoid shifting cash needed by the business to the profit pool. Report results quarterly, including individual shares. Either pay all annually or pay 30 percent to 50 percent of the profit sharing earned in the current quarter and the rest at year-end. The best plans make the first 50 percent firmly the employee's, without claw back. There are two motivators: the quarterly check, and the report of the company's profit pool progress with monthly financials. If possible, use a formula that allows all employees to calculate their potential share.

The only exception to such a plan is for salespeople who may be so driven by sales that they'll perform better with a commission plan. Do not cap it, because the more they sell, the more the company makes, if there's a gross margin "brake" on their commission, and they are only paid after each commission is fully collected.

◊ It's more believable to observe that all departments contribute to the profit from each order than to try to motivate people on individual or department performance. The logic is that no one employee in a company can function without the support of all the other employees. (If you have employees that aren't contributing, train or replace them, or eliminate their jobs.) Multiple plans invite disgruntled debates about favoritism. If you must pay incentive pay to departments or to salespeople, make a two-tier plan that's partly driven by their department and partly by company results.

◊ There is no holy grail. There is no perfect plan, so seek a strong plan, not a perfect one.

◊ Match their interests and aptitudes to their current position and future positions. Install a system that requires evaluation with every employee the match with current and planned next position every two years at least, if not annually. Replace the hackneyed annual performance system with this current and future match system. This requires:

» A baseline profile of each employee's interest and aptitudes.

» A system of matching and evaluating.

» A conversation with the leader and her leader about the next position for each employee, and one or two skills to consider when that position becomes available.

Use KPIs aggressively (see Chapter 3) to frame what is required to make the week and make the month.

Remarkably, this links to recent research about athletic performance. Key takeaway: Physical conditioning is essential, but world-class performers find another gear as they approach the finish line (end, target). That's in their heads, not their bodies.

The crucial first step is to accept the idea that your perceived capacity for endurance (or speed, or attention, etc.) doesn't always correspond to any physiological reality. The most compelling research example is a French study published in 2017 in *Medicine & Science in Sports & Exercise*.[7] Cyclists raced an avatar that they thought was set to match their best times. In fact, it was 2 percent faster, and they matched the new, faster time. When it was set 5 percent ahead, they couldn't keep up.[6]

Translation: You don't know what you're capable of, especially in bursts, and the end target (end of the race, end of the week at work) is essential to fuel the added performance.

Talent tip: Do you have your top two people in the highest-impact positions in the company? Those can be either permanent or temporary assignments. If not, what will it take to put them there?

The behavior that follows strong motivation is not the result of careful hiring (although it helps). It's a reflection of leadership that trains, recognizes, and appreciates excellent performance, and seeks to provide all three to every employee. If the pride of accomplishment doesn't provide motivation (and sometimes it doesn't), the recognition frequently will.

Chapter 10

Resilience

The beginning of wisdom is found in doubting. Pierre Abélard said, "By doubting we come to the question, and by seeking we may come upon the truth."[1]

The dreadful appeal of change is that it lets us look away from today's challenges to wonder into the future. The power is with today's demands, but the intellectual promise is about tomorrow, compounded by relief from today's intransigent dilemmas. If the answer is balance, how do the best accomplish that?

EXPECTING THE UNEXPECTED

Organizational resilience is informed response to the present, with a bit of good guessing about the future. Its foundation is execution; its future exploits execution and doubt to find opportunity. A surprise is always unplanned. The better way to deal with it is to build into

your organization the habits of responding to performance problems, with practiced escalation to strategy
when needed. Then the approached is planned, even if
the surprise is not.

The first answer, then, is to create brain space for
the unexpected, whatever it might be. Drop the dream
that there's a shortcut or that others can "see" the future
better than you. They can't. Here's a rule that's so simple, but most folks won't do it: Devote at least an hour
a day to reading, reflecting, or experimenting.

What does this look like? Here are the reading habits of famously successful folks:[1]

NAME	HOURS OF READING
Warren Buffett	twenty-five hours/week
Bill Gates	one book/week
Mark Zuckerberg	one book every other week
Elon Musk	two books/week
Mark Cuban	fifteen hours/week

To "devote" means to give something the attention that
you now award to the most precious thing or person in
your life. It's on your calendar with "Do not disturb" all
over it. If you struggle with this, your dilemma is plain:
You're running on empty. Although it's a common problem, it won't get you where you want to go, so stop it.
Do what successful people do to maintain their discipline: Fall in love with where you want to be so you can

enjoy the ride. After all, this is feeding your life. If you have trouble feeding your life, that's a second flag that you need to get help—a coach, a therapist, or a wise advisor who will help you build the walls to keep out the evil diversions.

There is no "fast track" to reading. Just pick up a book or a magazine or a newspaper with substance and start reading. Write notes in the margin when an idea strikes you. Some folks find that a daily log of learnings (phrases) or a weekly note to your key folks about what struck you in the current reading will pull you into reading because you've made an implicit promise to produce something with it. Your product is an idea, not necessarily a plan. It's called learning for its own sake. John Wooden, arguably the best coach in basketball, says "People with initiative will act when action is needed."[3] Harness your initiative and fear of failure to read and learn and doubt. It will open doors that you can't imagine.

The second answer for the uncertain future is to implant a culture that masters goals, budget, KPIs, and initiatives (GBKI) so that it can build a series of processes for managing the unexpected through the review and adjust meeting (RAM). That framework is universal and will travel to whatever business you develop. Without it, operational interruptions will suffocate the understanding that success requires. The heart of GBKI is the review and adjustment of meetings and actions that follow it.

Bar-tailed godwits fly 7,000 miles in eight or nine days straight from Alaska to New Zealand for their summer.

The real question is how they find their way, or how they adjust their path to stay headed at the target (RAM) because wind and weather likely push them off their planned daily path. The answer is an internal guidance system that uses Earth's magnetic field lines updated by positions of the sun, landmarks, and stars. That system combines magnetite (a mineral that acts like a magnet) in their bills with magnetosensitive eye molecules to sense the earth's magnetic field and then guide the birds back to the flight path.[4] If birds have a system to get back on the path daily, why don't all businesses, including yours?

Resilience Cycle

The review-and-adjust system does the same job for an organization that the godwit navigation system does for the birds' migration: It's a powerful way to make course corrections in the moment. The RAM produces planned actions that may improve results. If not, a second window

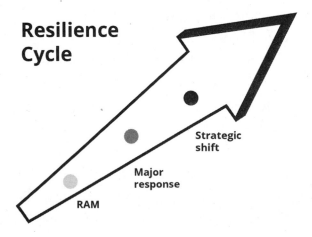

opens (major response), which suggests a deeper problem that may need more investment (people, time, machines, data) for a solution. When the deeper problem
recurs, a third window opens on the need for a strategic
revision. When to move up to the next window? When
frequent diversion or escalating risk occur. Trend data
matters here, requiring that a decision to act demands
more than one data point (except in an emergency, of
course).

Figure 10.2 below details the three stages driven by
the RAM to get back on course: RAM, major response,
strategic shift.

The resilience cycle, illustrated in Figure 10.3 on
page 216, is built on faithful execution of GBKI. Without it, leaders are at the mercy of their emotions or history, both lousy guides to a successful next step.

A strategic frame (plan) outlines a narrow set of
paths to success. Clear GBKI will point out good and
bad results, rapidly teeing up the questions that need

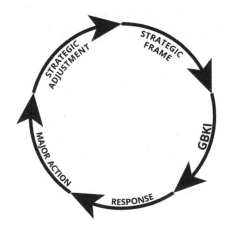

answers. Those questions lead to a RAM and subsequent actions. The task of leaders, especially at the top, is to assess whether the first actions from RAM are adequate. Frequently, either the problem or the solution will be new to the organization, which presents both opportunity for success now and a training exercise for unexpected problems in the future. All unanswered problems are unexpected, and solutions that work often require more than one try.

At Fort Dix, New Jersey, we taught new recruits how to use their gas masks. We walked to a small cement-block building, stopped, helped them prepare, and walked with them into (and then out of) the building, which contained a virulent blend of tear gas. Those with mask problems knew it immediately and scrambled out of the building nearly blind with tears. As soon as their vision cleared, they sat down to master wearing the mask before reentering the building. Everyone was required to master the mask, and nearly all did. The point is not that most mastered the task; it's the TCT process: try, check for proficiency, train, and repeat as needed (pictured in Figure 10.4 on page 219).

The number-one weakness in training (other than doing it) is in the checking. It's not that the checker knows how things should be done; it's how she or he checks that makes all the difference. The point of checking is to transfer knowledge to the trainee, not just to click the box on the checklist. If you find the air in a car tire is low, you've checked. Unless you refill the tire, you flunk.

It's what police and fire responders and surgeons do to master their craft and improve their performance. Don't miss the subtlety, though: They are rehearsing situations that are known possibilities but not yet encountered by them. That's not the same as situations that are new. "New" has a double meaning: I haven't experienced it, and neither has anyone in my organization, so we have limited data about it to help solve it. That multiplies the difficulty of mastery and raises the need for expert training.

This process seems obvious, but it is seldom practiced. A friend and emergency room physician moved after some years of medical practice to open one of the early brewpubs in Oakland, California. As he observed his top managers, he was floored: "As a physician I was taught: see it, do it, teach it. We weren't proficient until we'd demonstrated teaching proficiency in front of another physician. In business, there's little training,

it's not very specific, and there's little observation of hands-on performance until there's a problem!"

THE DIFFERENCE BETWEEN FEAR AND FORTUNE

The heavy breathing about courage ignores the reality that usually fear arrives before the courage, jamming our competence. Courage is doing what's needed despite fear. Instead of focusing on the fear to make it go away, the question is: How can one perform well while afraid?

A leader's main job is to make bets—on opportunities, people, machines, marketing campaigns, buildings, customers, and any three items that you can add to the list. Fear accompanies uncertainty when outcomes matter. Healthy people accept the real fear of disappointment and failure and learn to harness it toward the next success. Fear is a problem when it's the only tree in the forest, attracting compulsive circling to understand why you're afraid. "Why" is seldom helpful, and it perpetuates the myth that successful folks aren't ever afraid. The hundreds of top performers who are so afraid that they vomit before their performance include singers Adele and Beyoncé, soccer superstar Lionel Messi, and NBA legend Bill Russell.[5] Instead of the promise that "real leaders" aren't afraid, how about close attention to the people who find a way to perform even though afraid?

One way to reduce the odds of weak responses by fearful leaders is to bring fear right to the front porch of the business. A new technique explained by veteran futurist Bob Johansen is to go ten years out to the future and look back.[6] Forget about accurately forecasting ten years into the future or anything beyond twenty-four months. (Frankly, most forecasts beyond eighteen months make the forecasters feel good but are of little use.) The power in the ten-year look back is the set of answers to the real question: What should we be considering now, if this imagined future happens? The answers can be developed into an extension of the usual annual planning process, organized using these two steps.

Toolkit: Power Forecasting

Ask: Looking back from ten years into the future, what should we consider now?

Sort answers into two groups:

1. Topics with clear processes known by others, but not us, that we need to learn.

2. Topics that are new to us and most others, with unclear paths to manage them.

You've now built your roadmap into the new future.

Topics in the first group become potential action items to be prioritized with all others in the annual plan. Unless there is data marking it urgent, resist the urge to deeply and immediately jump into it. Instead, like most initiatives new to the organization, test a part of the response in a segment of the organization that will welcome the learning, be advocates for expanding it if justified, and will help teach it. If it seems urgent (significant progress needed this year), then move it to the top three business priorities, and act as you would with any top priority:

◊ Communicate its status and reason why to all employees.

◊ Expect supporting plans in each department to be presented to the management team.

◊ Review progress and method updates with the management team quarterly, on a schedule.

Topics in the second group are "new-new," and call for this approach:

◊ Sort by expected birth date: Will we need to respond in less than twenty-four months or more?

◊ Sort by expected impact on the business, even though these are best guesses.

If it requires action before twenty-four months and his high impact, move it to the top priority list and let it compete for top three.

Unexpected events will occur, their timing is sometimes a surprise, and parsing them with best current knowledge may make better responses available in a timely way. Fortune is a state of mind, more than any product or optimizing technique. It is opportunity married to healthy return, spurning shortcuts. Shortcuts usually cut short both the time and duration of the benefit, so serious folks take them off the table.

Much is made of the lean manufacturing revolution's explosive impact on the Toyota Motor Corporation. For Toyota, lean is a way of seeing and then acting. Here are two examples that are fundamental to the Toyota approach:

1. At hiring, every employee agrees to do the two required parts of their job daily:

    » Do their daily work.

    » Find ways to do that work better.

2. Early training for potential managers and engineers includes "a day of seeing":

    » Stand for a full shift in a marked place in a factory, not moving except for meals.

    » Note everything that happens.

    » Prepare to discuss what you've seen with your trainer.

Beyond the obvious expansion of "seeing," the investment of time and teaching communicates powerfully the value placed by the company in these skills. A corollary for leaders is that the most convincing way to teach priorities is an investment of time.

If that's Toyota's system for finding fortune, what's yours?

Toolkit: Results Multiplier

Here is a results multiplier to get you started. It peeks through a different window to highlight actions that will accelerate your results.

Expectations. Sloppy expectations are the root of friction between experienced employees and green folks. Experienced folks think that what's expected is obvious. New employees are often blind to the obvious for reasons beyond the control of experienced employees and managers. What to do? Spell out basic expectations, and check for them as a part of usual onboarding and accountability observations.

Accountability. Change your accountability expectation from catching mistakes to coaching excellence. The point of accountability checking is to clarify the next steps in performance improvement, and then assist in learning those new steps in the performance journey.

Expectation-driven people development. Expect managers to both deliver the numbers and to deliver

teams and individuals that share these expectations for themselves:

◊ They know what they need to do daily.

◊ They ask for help to do it on time and properly.

◊ They feel safe in recruiting their curiosity to find newer, better, simpler ways.

◊ They think it's their job to find opportunities for themselves and for the company.

IF EVERYTHING ALWAYS WENT RIGHT, WHO WOULD NEED YOU?

The unsettling truth is that successful organizations make changes because that's where the value is, whether it's solving a problem or developing a product. That means moving away from the way things are now. It's unsettling to realize that "we can't stay here," however, and it's made worse by our tendency to fear loss more than to desire gain.[7] Mistakes or falling short are a normal part of every change, every learning process. No one gets all the math problems right the first time (in fact, they are designed that way). Falling short is universally unpleasant, even in the healthiest folks, and the ability to restore progress toward the goal is vital. Two books of extensive studies about success and failure offer helpful paths to the success journey:

◊   *Grit* by Angela Duckworth documents the con-
     sistent hard work that success demands, along-
     side inevitable boredom, pain, and confusion.

◊   *Mindset* by Carol S. Dweck, PhD, explains the
     difference in mindset between people who
     think they can learn to do better, and folks who
     think they are stuck with who they are today.

The core finding of both books is that focused effort
beats talent. Yes, focused effort plus talent can equal
greatness, but those are outliers. The first response to
the feelings of disappointment, fear, confusion, and
doubt that come with falling short is either to deny them
or comfort them. Neither helps the people or solves
the problem. Instead, there is a three-step approach, a
problem reset that works for both optimists and pessi-
mists: acknowledge, normalize, fix.

Toolkit: The Problem Reset

Here are the three steps to the problem reset:

Acknowledge the problem. Say out loud something
like, "That didn't work." A speech isn't necessary, but
it is vital to say in front of the concerned folks that as
a leader you see that there's a problem. Otherwise, the
message for some is, "We don't talk about problems
here." In 2017, General Electric Corporation uncovered
system-wide problems that caused a precipitous drop
in their stock price, a substantial board reorganization,
major restructuring of the company, and more. The criticism was that top leaders didn't want to know about
problems, and discouraged discussion of them. That's

the opposite of what works. Problems mentioned usually can be evaluated and either resolved or dropped. Problems hidden will prompt a virus of other problems as they multiply in the darkness.

Normalize the problem. Remind your people that all change produces problems. There will be problems when the computer system goes down, when groups miss a key action, when the team is not prepared, and so on. Remind your team that problems can be fixed, that they have been fixed in the past, and they can be fixed this time too. This perspective balances acknowledgement of the shortcoming with a perspective of the future that is positive. It is sufficient for all but major catastrophe.

Fix it. Take a small step to begin to solve the problem or reduce the damage. Big problems can destabilize people, which dilutes their ability to think or act. Initiating small steps immediately will dilute the fear, reinforce feelings of competence, and usually,

will open the door to more comprehensive solutions. This feels counterintuitive because the big problem still looms, but unless there's an immediate solution that will completely restore order, the small-step approach will recruit the best skills and instincts of your people. At the same time, start the search for a permanent fix. Keep moving forward on both.

The best leaders balance the need for change with the need for predictability. "Need" is the right word. A significant fraction of folks mostly prefer consistency in their workplace and work assignments. And they often are the solid B players who are the foundation of a successful organization. They embrace change if it's presented clearly, well in advance, with modest and specific goals and expectations that they think they can either meet or learn. Their strengths are the cash generators and the launch point for successful growth. They include deep organizational knowledge, pride in doing good work, understanding of how to get things done, skills in their tasks and essential adjacencies (sometimes disparaged as tribal knowledge). Their appetite for change requires seasoning with preparation, training, personal relevance, and frank pictures of why the change is essential.

Media's thirst for drama feeds our fetish with unproven startups (AI, virtual reality), most of which will fail ("fail fast"). Valid in the search for dramatically new businesses, their example of unhinged change is a poor matrix for successful growth. The undramatic truth is that most successful firms grow modestly but relentlessly.

Real business power is fueled by relentless performance because customer re-purchase (the prime metric of successful growth) is about customer satisfaction, not the whiz-bang of the technology.

The formula for successful change leadership looks like this:

1. Institutionalize the search for change.

2. Expect results.

3. Create solid linkage with existing people and processes.

4. Maintain consistent recognition and stimulation of existing practices and people.

Today's examples of this formula include both Facebook and 3M, even though they are radically different from each other.

THE FUTURE IS NOW

Robert MacLellan, cofounder of the remarkably successful Pacific Coast Restaurant chain, explains how it all started: After a Navy career as a petty officer, where he learned how effective training and disciplined execution live together, he and his three partners were invited to open a Wendy's franchise in Medford, Oregon. They did so with a bang: Sales and profit grew to triple the national average for the chain! Wendy's founder, Dave Thomas, flew to Medford from Ohio in his company plane to see it. Although built upon many details, including extreme care in hiring, these principles stand out:

Close control of costs. The high volume and low margins in the fast food business demand exemplary cost control, especially in food cost and labor. Relentless focus on both became a foundation of their business. According to Robert McLellan, "You drop a little cheese on the floor, there goes your profit."

Collapse slow points (CSP). In one year, they reduced the time for a customer to get a hamburger from the company standard sixty seconds down to thirteen seconds. Each. For an entire meal shift, lunch or dinner. How? By identifying slow points in the process, looking closely at ways to reduce their times, and teaching their people how to do it. Not only were there lines out to the street (partly because people wanted to experience it), but the cars never stopped rolling! Servers with headsets walked up the line taking orders and sending them to the kitchen.[8]

Surprise customers with powerful value. The point of the speed and cost control was a quicker good lunch. Customers liked it so well they lined up for it. That's value.

What does this have to do with the idea that the future is now? Robert's team didn't wait for the future to come to them. They understood that there is no such thing as the future. There is only now. The future is an accounting device that totals up the nows. A bit of Janus, the Roman god of transitions whose two faces looked forward to the future and back to the past, applies here: Look to the future to inform actions now, when it matters. What future can your now provide?

Before you object that your business is different from Wendy's (of course it is), ask yourself: Would you like to triple your profit? That's what Robert's team did in a year in Medford. Your results may vary, but the odds are with you if you'll try this tool.

Emphasize the total result, not any one process. Whenever you make a process change, check the impact on your customer, not just the change at the slow point. If the change is invisible at the shipping dock or the delivery point, move to another slow point. High-leverage improvements like cost control or CSP can crush your competition with superior offerings in quality, packaging, personal service, or even price. The idea is to invest the savings into two pockets: profit and customer value. Done right, it's included in the training and accountability systems that already exist. In fact, price may be the last thing that you change, unless you move it up.

Too often, attempts at cost control and faster delivery descend into cost cutting (quality cutting) tacked on to a work speed-up. Both are the wrong approach. Unless an improved process enables faster throughput, speed boosts waste and the chance for injury and quality busts; speed becomes the enemy. Instead, step up to the courage plate and ask your team to collapse slow points anywhere in your entire process, from order to delivery.

Toolkit: Collapse Slow Points (CSP)

1. Recruit your best slow-point collapsers to teach others what to look for.

2. Ask them to pick a slow point.

3. Arm them with a few good questions to speed the search.

4. Spell out the collapse point and the fix.

5. Build in training for the new methods so your people can do them easily.

6. Track and proclaim the results weekly, preferably to all in the company.

7. Ask the final question: How can we translate this into better customer experience?

For Wendy's in Medford, the improved experience was service so fast that folks came to see it and stayed to buy. The power in CSP is to increase both profit and value for the customer, chosen so that it matters to the customer.

"Now" Is a Business Stance

The power of now isn't speed; it's offerings that click neatly into customers' wants, even before they know they want it. Speed is not enough. What wins is best summarized as value: something customers will pay for, delivered quickly.

Menswear retailer Bonobos is successful not because they're on the web or because of their prices;

they are not cheap. They win because they solve these problems:

◊   Men (like me) hate to shop.

◊   Men hate their pants. (According to research done by founder Brian Spaly with business school classmates and others.)

The Bonobos formula offers pants and clothes that fit, good selection, quick shopping, and prepaid returns. GuideShops offer a brick-and-and mortar place for a customer to reserve a time with an expert who will help find clothes that the customer prefers, see that they fit, and ship them to the customer at home. The clincher is its insistence that their customer service "ninjas" be human with their customers, treat them like people, think what they would want if they were in the customer's shoes, and then do that without fear of recrimination. It's the Nordstrom formula strapped to Internet speed.[9]

PERSONAL RESILIENCE

Self-care for leaders is vital. Always. The memory of an all-nighter is destructive because it promotes work that's late and lousy. If I imagine an all-nighter to resolve today's problems, my fantasy will prevent pruning priorities to the success core. The payoff for self-care is that you're present enough in your now to have a chance at success. Here are your first four examples of self-care:

Humble leadership. Leaders still lead, but with humility that owns the real possibility that they might be wrong and that they will learn from others. They don't need to be right all the time, and they'll do better if they aren't. Humble leadership doesn't dilute the urgency to act. Instead, this state of mind creates space for reality to emerge and encourages others to step up and into it. Instead of rejecting an idea that seems wrong, ask, "Why do you think that?"

Deep personal relationships. "Loneliness kills," according to Harvard psychiatrist Robert Waldinger, current head of the Harvard Study of Adult Development, a one-of-a-kind eighty-year continuing study of physical and mental health of more than 2,000 men. People who have one or two close personal relationships for much of their lives will do better by virtually all measures than those who don't. These relationships can be marriage, friendships, at work, outside work, or beyond work. Let them grow deep over time. How to do it? If you have it, keep it. If you don't, start looking for folks that you enjoy and that wear well over time. Regularly spend some time with them. (For more on this topic, find Dr. Waldinger's TED Talk, "What Makes a Good Life? Lessons from the Longest Study on Happiness.")

Hope. A hopeful life stance isn't Pollyanna weakness. It fuels the vitality that draws organizations and people into their next challenge with a growing chance of success. Says psychologist Martin Seligman, PhD, "Believing that you have some control over what happens fuels trying. If there's a potentially good event for me, I'm going to seize the opportunity and follow up."[10] Hope doesn't always have to be successful, but it increases the odds of success.

Persistence. This is especially important when trying new ways to get to your answer. Caltech physicist Leonard Mlodinow says, "You have to keep trying and accepting failure, because the more at-bats you have, the more likely you are to get a hit."[11] Persistence has been glorified in every success story, regardless of where it happened. Why not grab it for yourself? How many successful people have bragged about how little persistence their success required? Even notorious bank robber Al Capone robbed multiple banks. Why do you think the world will treat you differently?

The secret of a resilient organization, then, is practice in spotting problems and opportunities, and jumping on the ones that matter in the present. That capability becomes resilience when surprises show up, and they will. The secret of personal resilience is a solid mix of hope, a few close relationships, humble willingness to seize failure as painful opportunity, and dogged persistence. And the greatest of these is persistence. All four are available at your door, now.

Acknowledgments

I t's here that I face my limits. This thank you looks inadequate as I reflect on your help with this book. So, my deep thanks and admiration for your skill and discipline.

Thank you to my mentor Alan Weiss, whose insights helped frame this book and support my writing it; my editor, Nina Taylor, a remarkable safety blanket that Linus would envy; and copy thinker–marketing whiz Jerry Fletcher.

Thanks also to the five generous leaders who shared some of their stories with me, and with this book. They picked up the pace and colored the picture: Nautilus CEO Bruce Cazenave, Restaurant guru Robert Maclellan, Oregon Symphony CEO Scott Showalter, Adelsheim Winery CEO Joth Ricci, and Triad Speakers founder Larry Pexton. Each has delivered creatively remarkable results in the businesses they have led and worked in. Their insights are authentic.

Special thanks to my clients, whose willingness to work with me has taught me much of what you'll find in this book. They relentlessly seek what works.

I especially want to thank my wife (and night psychiatrist) Leslie Neilson, MD, for hundreds of pithy insights that make me look wiser than I am and for the kind of marriage and support that books are written about.

Finally, thanks to friends and mentors including Rick Pay, Phil Symchych, Manoj Garg, Heidi Pozzo, Jerry Vieira, Bruce Hazen, and Norm Duffett, among many. This joint effort is the better for all of them.

Notes

Chapter 1

1. Martin Laird, *Into the Silent Land* (Oxford: Oxford University Press, 2006), 7, 19.
2. Richard L. Byyny, "Cognitive Bias: Recognizing and Managing Our Unconscious Bias," *The Pharos* (Winter 2017), 2.
3. The Vegetarian Resource Group, "How Many Adults in America Are Vegetarian or Vegan?" *www.vrg.org*
4. Ryan Mac, "Professor Billionaire: The Stanford Academic Who Wrote Google Its First Check," *Forbes.com*, August 1, 2012.

Chapter 2

1. Mary Beth Steinfeld, MD, "Bonding Is Essential for Normal Human Development," UC Davis Medical

Center, *https://www.ucdmc.ucdavis.edu/medical center/healthtips/20100114_infant-bonding.html*

2. "Group Dynamics and Behavior," *Understanding and Changing the Social World,* *https://doi. org/10.24926/8668.2401*

3. Prudy Gourgechon, "Empathy Is an Essential Leadership Skill—And There's Nothing Soft About It," *Forbes.com,* December 26, 2017.

4. Gourgechon, "Empathy."

5. Gourgechon, "Empathy."

6. Yudhijit Bahattacharjee, "The Science of Good and Evil," *National Geographic,* January 2018, 131–142.

7. Timothy Gallwey, *The Inner Game of Tennis* (New York: Random House, 1974), 96–97.

8. Bob Johansen, *The New Leadership Literacies* (Oakland, CA: Berrett-Koehler, 2017), 34.

9. Christopher Voss, *Never Split the Difference* (New York: HarperCollins, 2016), various pages.

CHAPTER 3

1. Thomas Sowell, @ThomasSowell, Twitter, November 24, 2017.

2. Daniel Kahneman, *Thinking, Fast and Slow* (New York: Farrar, Straus and Giroux, 2011), 417.

3. Thomas Sowell, @ThomasSowell, Twitter, September 28, 2015.

4. Bryce Hoffman, *American Icon: Alan Mulally and the Fight to Save Ford Motor Company* (New York: Crown Business, 2012), 124–125.

5. Alan Mulally on *The Marshall Goldsmith Thinkers 50 Video Blog,* January 8, 2018, *http://thinkers50. com/sharing/marshall-goldsmith-video-blog/*

CHAPTER 4

1. Marshall Goldsmith, "Lessons I Learned from the Father of Modern Management, Peter Drucker," *MarshallGoldsmith.com*
2. This approach is from Joth Ricci, serial CEO/president, and builder of successful organizations including Stumptown Coffee, interview, January 4, 2018.
3. Lewis Howes, "10 Lessons for Entrepreneurs from Coach John Wooden," *Forbes.com,* October 19, 2012.
4. Carolyn Wood, *Tough Girl* (Portland, OR: White Pine Press, 2016).
5. Larry Pexton, interview, March 7, 2018.
6. Don Peppers, "The Downside of Six Sigma," *LinkedIn. com,* May 5, 2016,
7. Geoff Colvin, "How Intuit Reinvents Itself," *Fortune. com,* October 20, 2017, 79ff.

CHAPTER 5

1. Jon Cooper, "Top 50 Quotes from Bear Bryant," *SaturdayDownSouth.com.*
2. Claudia Kalb, "What Makes a Genius?" *National Geographic,* May 2017, 54.

CHAPTER 6

1. Voss, *Never Split the Difference,* 17.
2. Johansen, *The New Leadership Literacies,* 34.
3. Sue Vorenberg, "A Conductor of All Things Business," *Portland Business Journal,* April 21, 2017, 27.
4. Scott Showalter, interview, November 10, 2017.
5. Bruce Cazenave, interview, December 15, 2017.

CHAPTER 7

1. Ty Kiisel, "82 Percent of People Don't Trust the Boss to Tell the Truth," *Forbes.com,* January, 30, 2013.
2. Ty Kiisel, "65 Percent of Americans Choose a Better Boss Over a Raise—Here's Why," *Forbes.com,* October 16, 2012.
3. Tom Junod, "Can You Say . . . Here?" *Esquire.com,* April 6, 2017 (Originally published in *Esquire,* November 1998).
4. Oren Harari, "Quotations from Chairman Powell: A Leadership Primer," *www.govleaders.org*
5. Joth Ricci, interview, January 4, 2018.
6. Sally French, "People Waited in Line 5 Hours for Disney's 5-Minute Frozen Ride," *MarketWatch.com,* June 28, 2016.

CHAPTER 8

1. Benjamine Tregoe and John Zimmerman, *Top Management Strategy* (New York: Simon & Schuster, 1980), 43.

2. Ibid.

3. Sarah Vowell, "A University of, by and for the People," Sunday Review, *New York Times,* February 15, 2018.

4. Salt and Straw, *https://saltandstraw.com/flavors/#portland*

5. Julia Reed, "The Gospel According to Oprah," *Wall Street Journal Magazine,* February 12, 2018.

· CHAPTER 9

1. Anna Wilde Matthews, Emily Glazer, and Laura Stevens, "Triple Threat: Amazon, Berkshire, JP Morgan Rattle Health-Care Firms," *Wall Street Journal,* January 30, 2018, 1ff.

2. Dylan Walsh, "Look Beyond 'Culture Fit' When Hiring," Insights by Stanford Business, *www.gsb.stanford.edu,* February 1, 2018.

3. Walsh, "Hiring."

4. *LeanIn.org,* "4 Things All Mentors and Mentees Should Know," *www.LeanIn.org/tips/mentorship*

5. Robbie Whelan, "Billionaire Carlos Slim Gets Schooled by an Old Pupil," *Wall Street Journal,* January 30, 2018, A1.

6. Ken Blanchard and Spencer Johnson, *The One Minute Manager* (New York: HarperCollins, 1981), 44.

7. P. G. Bell, M. J. Furber, K. A. Van Someren, A. Antón-Solanas, and J. Swart, "The Physiological Profile of a Multiple Tour de France Winning Cyclist," *Medicine & Science in Sports & Exercise,* 49(1):115–123.

8. Alex Hutchinson, "The Mental Tricks of Athletic Endurance," *Wall Street Journal,* February 6, 2018, C2.

CHAPTER 10

1. Bookshelf, *Wall Street Journal,* March 3, 2018, C8.
2. Mark Simmons, "Bill Gates, Warren Buffet, and Oprah All Use the 5-Hour Rule—Here's How It Works," *BusinessInsider.com,* July 10, 2017.
3. John Wooden and Jay Carty, *Coach Wooden's Pyramid of Success* (Ada, MI: Revell, 2005), 58.
4. Yudhijit Bhattacharjee, "Epic Migrations," *National Geographic,* March 2018, 42–51.
5. J. Francis Wolfe, "Top 15 Athletes Who Literally Get Sick Before Games," *TheSportster.com,* February 24, 2017.
6. Johansen, *The New Leadership Literacies,* 34.
7. Kahneman, *Thinking, Fast and Slow,* 417.
8. Robert MacLellan, interview, March 1, 2018.
9. Sam Parr, "How the Bonobos Founder Went from 'Insufficient ATM Funds' to Over $100 Million in Revenue," *The Hustle, Hustle.com,* February 25, 2016.
10. Janice Kaplan and Barnaby Marsh, "To Be Successful, Make Your Own Luck," *Wall Street Journal,* March 4, 2018, C3.
11. Kaplan and Marsh, "To Be Successful," C3.

Index